Anatomy of Reality

ANATOMY OF REALITY
Merging of Intuition and Reason

Jonas Salk

CONVERGENCE
A Series Founded, Planned, and Edited by Ruth Nanda Anshen

Praeger

PRAEGER SPECIAL STUDIES • PRAEGER SCIENTIFIC

New York • Philadelphia • Eastbourne, UK
Toronto • Hong Kong • Tokyo • Sydney

Library of Congress Cataloging in Publication Data

Salk, Jonas, 1914—
    Anatomy of reality.

    (Convergence)
    Reprint. Originally published: New York : Columbia University Press, 1983.
    1. Science—Philosophy. 2. Reality. 3. Intuition. 4. Reason. I. Title. II. Series: Convergence (New York, N.Y.)
[Q175.S2326 1985]   128   84—17920
ISBN 0—03—001013—6 (alk. paper)

Published and Distributed by the
Praeger Publishers Division
(ISBN Prefix 0-275)
of Greenwood Press, Inc.,
Westport, Connecticut

Published in 1985 by Praeger Publishers
CBS Educational and Professional Publishing
a Division of CBS Inc.
521 Fifth Avenue, New York, NY 10175 USA
© 1983 by Jonas Salk
"Convergence" and "The Möbius Strip"
© 1981 by Ruth Nanda Anshen

All rights reserved

56789 052 987654321

Printed in the United States of America
on acid-free paper

To the well-trodden paths of ancient wisdom,
To the unfolding of universal evolution,
To Ruth Nanda Anshen, who made this book a reality.

CONVERGENCE
A Series Founded, Planned, and Edited by Ruth Nanda Anshen

Board of Editors

Sir Fred Hoyle
Sir Bernard Lovell
Adolph Lowe
Joseph Needham
I. I. Rabi
William Richardson
Jonas Salk
Lewis Thomas
C. N. Yang

Books in the Convergence Series

The Double-Edged Helix
Genetic Engineering in the Real World
Liebe F. Cavalieri

Progress or Catastrophe
The Nature of Biological Science and Its Impact on Human Society
Bentley Glass

Emerging Cosmology
Bernard Lovell

Creation and Evolution
Myth or Reality?
Norman D. Newell

Anatomy of Reality
Merging of Intuition and Reason
Jonas Salk

Science and Moral Priority
Merging Mind, Brain, and Human Values
Roger Sperry

CONTENTS

CONVERGENCE Ruth Nanda Anshen	xi
THE MÖBIUS STRIP R.N.A.	xxv
ACKNOWLEDGMENTS	xxvii
INTRODUCTION	1

PERCEPTION
Discovery	7
Human Mind in Evolution	12
The Great Mystery	16
Process	20
Conceptual Maps	23

NATURE
Matter	35
Anatomy of Matter	39
Dynamic Asymmetry	42
Relationship	44
Context and Substance	48

EVOLUTION
Universal Evolution	53
Biological and Metabiological Evolution	58
Creativity	63
Human Experience	66
Criteria for Selection	69
Consciousness of Evolution	72

MIND
Emergence of Mind	77
Intuition and Reason	79
Unitary Vision	81
Values—Individual and Societal	83
The Evolutionary Path	87
Our Sensory System	90
Influences on Mind	93
Metabiological Health	98

EMERGENCE
The Problem	103
A New Cosmogony	107
Individual Mutualism	109
Conscious Evolution	111
The Present	113
The New Reality	122

ABOUT THE AUTHOR   125

ABOUT THE FOUNDER OF THIS SERIES   127

CONVERGENCE
by
Ruth Nanda Anshen

"There is no use trying," said Alice; "one *can't* believe impossible things."

"I dare say you haven't had much practice," said the Queen. "When I was your age, I always did it for half an hour a day. Why, sometimes I've believed as many as six impossible things before breakfast."

This commitment is an inherent part of human nature and an aspect of our creativity. Each advance of science brings increased comprehension and appreciation of the nature, meaning, and wonder of the creative forces that move the cosmos and created man. Such openness and confidence lead to faith in the reality of possibility and eventually to the following truth: "The mystery of the universe is its comprehensibility."

When Einstein uttered that challenging statement, he could have been speaking about our relationship with the universe. The old division of the Earth and the Cosmos into objective processes in space and time and mind in which they are mirrored is no longer a suitable starting point for understanding the universe, science, or ourselves. Science now begins to focus on the convergence of man and nature, on the framework which makes us, as living beings, dependent parts of nature and simultaneously makes nature the object of our thoughts and actions. Scientists can no longer confront the universe as objective observers. Science recognizes the participation of man with the universe. Speaking quantitatively, the universe is largely indifferent to what happens in man. Speaking qualitatively, nothing happens in man that does not have a bearing on the elements which constitute the universe. This gives cosmic significance to the person.

Nevertheless, all facts are not born free and equal. There exists a hierarchy of facts in relation to a hierarchy of values. To arrange the facts rightly, to differentiate the important from the trivial, to see their bearing in relation to each other and to evaluational criteria, requires a judgment which is intuitive as well as empirical. Man needs meaning in addition to information. Accuracy is not the same as truth.

Our hope is to overcome the cultural *hubris* in which we have been living. The scientific method, the technique of analyzing, explaining, and classifying, has demonstrated its inherent limitations. They arise because, by its intervention, science presumes to alter and fashion the object of its investigation. In reality, method and object can no longer be separated. The outworn Cartesian, scientific world view has ceased to be scientific in the most profound sense of the word, for a common bond links us all—man, animal, plant, and galaxy—in the unitary principle of all reality. For the self without the universe is empty.

This universe of which we human beings are particles may be defined as a living, dynamic process of unfolding. It is a breathing universe, its respiration being only one of the many rhythms of its life. It is evolution itself. Although what we observe may seem to be a community of separate, independent units, in actuality these units are made up of subunits, each with a life of its own, and the subunits constitute smaller living entities. At no level in the hierarchy of nature is independence a reality. For that which lives and constitutes matter, whether organic or inorganic, is dependent on discrete entities that, gathered together, form aggregates of new units which interact in support of one another and become an unfolding event, in constant motion, with ever-increasing complexity and intricacy of their organization.

Are there goals in evolution? Or are there only discernible patterns? Certainly there is a law of evolution by which we can explain the emergence of forms capable of activities which are indeed novel. Examples may be said to be the origin of life, the emergence of individual consciousness, and the appearance of language.

The hope of the concerned authors in Convergence is that they will show that evolution and development are interchangeable and that the entire system of interweaving of man, nature, and the universe constitutes a living totality. Man is searching for his legitimate place in this unity, this cosmic scheme of things. The meaning of this cosmic scheme—if indeed we can impose meaning on the mystery and majesty of nature—and the extent to which we can assume responsibility in it as uniquely intelligent beings, are supreme questions for which this Series seeks an answer.

Inevitably, toward the end of a historical period, when thought and custom have petrified into rigidity and when the elaborate machinery of civilization opposes and represses our more noble qualities, life stirs again beneath the hard surface. Nevertheless, this attempt to define the purpose of Convergence is set forth with profound trepidation. We are living in a period of extreme darkness. There is moral atrophy, destructive radiation within us, as we watch the collapse of values hitherto cherished—but now betrayed. We seem to be face to face with an apocalyptic destiny. The anomie, the chaos, surrounding us produces an almost lethal disintegration of the person, as well as ecological and demographic disaster. Our situation is desperate. And there is no glossing over the deep and unresolved tragedy that fills our lives. Science now begins to question its premises and tells us not only what *is*, but what *ought* to be; *pre*scribing in addition to *de*scribing the realities of life, reconciling order and hierarchy.

My introduction to Convergence is not to be construed as a prefatory essay to each individual volume. These few pages attempt to set forth the general aim and purpose of this Series. It is my hope that this statement will provide the reader with a new orientation in his thinking, one more specifically defined by these scholars who have been invited to participate in this intellectual, spiritual, and moral endeavor so desparately needed in our time. These scholars recognize the relevance of the nondiscursive experience of life which the discursive, analytical method alone is unable to convey.

The authors invited to Convergence Series acknowledge a structural kinship between subject and object, between living and nonliving matter, the immanence of the past energizing the present and thus bestowing a promise for the future. This kinship has long been sensed and experienced by mystics. Saint Francis of Assisi described with extraordinary beauty the truth that the more we know about nature, its unity with all life, the more we realize that we are one family, summoned to acknowledge the intimacy of our familial ties with the universe. At one time we were so anthropomorphic as to exclude as inferior such other aspects of our relatives as animals, plants, galaxies, or other species—even inorganic matter. This only exposed our provincialism. Then we believed there were borders beyond which we could not, must not, trespass. These frontiers have never existed. Now we are beginning to recognize, even take pride in, our neighbors in the Cosmos.

Human thought has been formed through centuries of man's consciousness, by perceptions and meanings that relate us to nature. The smallest living entity, be it a molecule or a particle, is at the same time present in the structure of the Earth and all its inhabitants, whether human or manifesting themselves in the multiplicity of other forms of life.

Today we are beginning to open ourselves to this evolved experience of consciousness. We keenly realize that man has intervened in the evolutionary process. The future is contingent, not completely prescribed, except for the immediate necessity to evaluate in order to live a life of integrity. The specific gravity of the burden of change has moved from genetic to cultural evolution. Genetic evolution itself has taken millions of years; cultural evolution is a child of no more than twenty or thirty thousand years. What will be the future of our evolutionary course? Will it be cyclical in the classical sense? Will it be linear in the modern sense? Yet we know that the laws of nature are not linear. Certainly, life is more than mere endless repetition. We must restore the importance of each moment, each deed. This is impossible if the future is nothing but a mechanical extrapolation of the past. Dignity becomes possible only with choice. The choice is ours.

In this light, evolution shows man arisen by a creative power inherent in the universe. The immense ancestral effort that has borne man invests him with a cosmic responsibility. Michelangelo's image of Adam created at God's command becomes a more intelligent symbol of man's position in the world than does a description of man as a chance aggregate of atoms or cells. Each successive stage of emergence is more comprehensive, more meaningful, more fulfilling, and more converging, than the last. Yet a higher faculty must always operate through the levels that are below it. The higher faculty must enlist the laws controlling the lower levels in the service of higher principles, and the lower level which enables the higher one to operate through it will always limit the scope of these operations, even menacing them with possible failure. All our higher endeavors must work through our lower forms and are necessarily exposed thereby to corruption. We may thus recognize the cosmic roots of tragedy and our fallible human condition. Language itself, as the power of universals, is the basic expression of man's ability to transcend his environment and to transmute tragedy into a moral and spiritual triumph.

This relationship, this convergence, of the higher with the lower applies again when an upper level, such as consciousness or freedom, endeavors to reach beyond itself. If no higher level can be accounted for by the operation of a lower level, then no effort can be accounted for by the operation of a lower level, then no effort of ours can be truly creative in the sense of establishing a higher principle not intrinsic to our initial condition. And establishing such a principle is what all great art, great thought, and great action must aim at. This is indeed how these efforts have built up the heritage in which our lives continue to grow.

Has man's intelligence broken through the limits of his own powers? Yes and no. Inventive efforts can never fully account for their success, but the story of man's evolution testifies to a creative power that goes beyond that which we can account for in ourselves. This power can make us surpass ourselves. We exercise some of it in the simple act of acquiring knowledge and holding it to be true. For, in doing so, we strive for intellectual control over things outside ourselves, in spite of our manifest incapacity to justify this hope. The greatest efforts of the human mind amount to no more than this. All such acts impose an obligation to strive for the ostensibly impossible, representing man's search for the fulfillment of those ideals which, for the moment, seem to be beyond his reach. For the good of a moral act is inherent in the act itself and has the power to ennoble the person who performs it. Without this moral ingredient there is corruptiion.

The origins of one person can be envisaged by tracing that person's family tree all the way back to the primeval specks of protoplasm in which his first origins lie. The history of the family tree converges with everything that has contributed to the making of a human being. This segment of evolution is on a par with the history of a fertilized egg developing into a mature person, or the history of a plant growing from a seed; it includes everything that caused that person, or that plant, or that animal, or even that star in a galaxy, to come into existence. Natural selection plays no part in the evolution of a single human being. We do not include in the mechanism of growth the possible adversities which did not befall it and hence did not prevent it. The same principle of development holds for evolution of a single human being; nothing is gained in understanding this evolution by considering the adverse chances which might have prevented it.

In our search for a reasonable cosmic view, we turn in the

first place to common understanding. Science largely relies for its subject matter on a common knowledge of things. Concepts of life and death, plant and animal, health and sickness, youth and age, mind and body, machine and technical processes, and other innumerable and equally important things are commonly known. All these concepts apply to complex entities, whose reality is called into question by a theory of knowledge which claims that the entire universe should ultimately be represented in all its aspects by the physical laws governing the inanimate substrate of nature. "Technological inevitability" has alienated man's relationship with nature, with other human beings, with himself. Judgment, decision, and freedom of choice, in other words *knowledge* which contains a moral imperative, cannot be ordered in the form that some technological scientists believe. For there is no mechanical ordering, no exhaustive set of permutations or combinations that can perform the task. The power which man has achieved through technology has been transformed into spiritual and moral impotence. Without the insight into the nature of *being*, more important than *doing*, the soul of man is imperilled. And those self-transcendent ends that ultimately confer dignity, meaning and identity on man and his life constitute the only final values worth pursuing. The pollution of consciousness is the result of mere technological efficiency. In addition, the authors in this Series recognize that the computer in itself can process information—not meaning. Thus we see on the stage of life no moral actors, only anonymous events.

Our new theory of knowledge, as the authors in this Series try to demonstrate, rejects this claim and restores our respect for the immense range of common knowledge acquired by our experience of convergence. Starting from here, we sketch out our cosmic perspective by exploring the wider implications of the fact that all knowledge is acquired and possessed by relationship, coalescence, convergence.

We identify a person's physiognomy by depending on our awareness of features that we are unable to specify, and this amounts to a convergence in the features of a person for the purpose of comprehending their joint meaning. We are also able to read in the features and behavior of a person the presence of moods, the gleam of intelligence, the response to animals or a sunset or a fugue by Bach, the signs of sanity, human responsibility, and experience. At a lower level, we comprehend by a similar mechanism the body of a person and understand the functions of the physiological mechanism. We know that even physical theories constitute in this way the processes of inanimate nature. Such are the various levels of knowledge acquired and possessed by the experience of convergence.

The authors in this Series grasp the truth that these levels form a hierarchy of comprehensive entities. Inorganic matter is comprehended by physical laws; the mechanism of physiology is built on these laws and enlists them in its service. Then, the intelligent behavior of a person relies on the healthy functions of the body and, finally, moral responsibility relies on the faculties of intelligence directing moral acts.

We realize how the operations of machines, and of mechanisms in general, rely on the laws of physics but cannot be explained, or accounted for, by these laws. In a hierarchic sequence of comprehensive levels, each higher level is related to the levels below it in the same way as the operations of a machine are related to the particulars, obeying the laws of physics. We cannot explain the operations of an upper level in terms of the particulars on which its operations rely. Each higher level of integration represents, in this sense, a higher level of existence, not completely accountable by the levels below it yet including these lower levels implicitly.

In a hierarchic sequence of comprehensive levels each higher level is known to us by relying on our awareness of the particulars on the level below it. We are conscious of each level by internalizing its particulars and mentally performing the integration that constitutes it. This is how all experience, as well as all knowledge, is based on convergence, and this is how the consecutive stages of convergence form a continuous transition from the understanding of the inorganic, the inanimate, to the comprehension of man's moral responsibility and participation in the totality, the organismic whole, of all reality. The sciences of the subject-object relationship thus pass imperceptibly into the metascience of the convergence of the subject and object interrelationship, mutually altering each other. From the minimum of convergence, exercised in a physical observation, we move without a break to the maximum of convergence, which is a total commitment.

"The last of life, for which the first was made, is yet to come." Thus, Convergence has summoned the world's most concerned thinkers to rediscover the experience of *feeling*, as well as of thought. The convergence of all forms of reality presides over the possible fulfillment of self-awareness—not the isolated, alienated self, but rather the participation in the life process with other lives and other forms of live. Convegence is a cosmic force and may possess liberating powers allowing man to become what he is, capable of freedom, justice, love. Thus man experiences the meaning of grace.

A further aim of this Series is not, nor could it be, to disparage science. The authors themselves are adequate witness to this fact. Actually, in viewing the role of science, one arrives at a much more modest judgment of its function in our whole body of knowledge. Original knowledge was probably not acquired by us in the active sense; most of it must have been given to us in the same mysterious way we received our consciousness. As to content and usefulness, scientific knowledge is an infinitesimal fraction of natural knowledge. Nevertheless, it is knowledge whose structure is endowed with beauty because its abstractions satisfy our urge for specific knowledge much more fully than does natural knowledge, and we are justly proud of scientific knowledge because we can call it our own creation. It teaches us clear thinking, and the extent to which clear thinking helps us to order our sensations is a marvel which fills the mind with ever new and increasing admiration and awe. Science now begins to include the realm of human values, lest even the memory of what it means to be human be forgotten.

Organization and energy are always with us, wherever we look, on all levels. At the level of the atom organization becomes indistinguishable from form, from order, from whatever the forces are that hold the spinning groups of ultimate particles together in their apparent solidity. And now that we are at the atomic level, we find that modern physics has recognized that these ultimate particles are primarily electrical charges, and that mass is therefore a manifestation of energy. This has often been misinterpreted by idealists as meaning that matter has somehow been magicked away as if by a conjuror's wand. But nothing could be more untrue. It is impossible to transform matter into spirit just by making it thin. Bishop Berkeley's views admit of no refutation but carry no conviction nevertheless. However, something has happened to matter. It was only separated from form because it seemed too simple. Now we realize that—and this is a revolutionary change—we cannot separate them. We are now summoned to cease speaking of Form and Matter and begin to consider the convergence of Organization and Energy. For the largest molecule we know and the smallest living particles we know overlap. Such a cooperation, even though far down at the molecular level, cannot but remind us of the voluntary cooperation of individual human beings in maintaining patterns of society at levels of organization far higher. The tasks of Energy and Organization in the making of the universe and ourselves are far from ended.

No individual destiny can be separated from the destiny of the universe. Alfred North Whitehead has stated that every event, every step or process in the universe, involves both effects from past situations and the anticipation of future potentialities. Basic for this doctrine is the assumption that the course of the universe results from a multiple and never-ending complex of steps developing out of one another. Thus, in spite of all evidence to the contrary, we conclude that there is a continuing and permanent energy of that which is not only man but all of life. For not an atom stirs in matter, organic and inorganic, that does not have its cunning duplicate in mind. And faith in the convergence of life with all its multiple manifestations creates its own verification.

We are concerned in this Series with the unitary structure of all nature. At the beginning, as we see in Hesiod's *Theogony* and in the Book of Genesis, there was a primal unity, a state of fusion in which, later, all elements become separated but then merge again. However, out of this unity there emerge, through separation, parts of opposite elements. These opposites intersect or reunite, in meteoric phenomena or in individual living things. Yet, in spite of the immense diversity of creation, a profound underlying convergence exists in all nature. And the principle of the conservation of energy simply signifies that there is a *something* that remains constant. Whatever fresh notions of the world may be given to us by future experiments, we are certain beforehand that something remains unchanged which we call *energy*. We now do not say that the law of nature springs from the invariability of God, but with that curious mixture of arrogance and humility which scientists have learned to put in place of theological terminology, we say instead that the law of conservation is the physical expression of the elements by which nature makes itself understood by us.

The universe is our home. There is no other universe than the universe of all life including the mind of man, the merging of life with life. Our consciousness is evolving, the primordial principle of the unfolding of that which is implied or contained in all matter and spirit. We ask: Will the central mystery of the cosmos, as well as man's awareness of and participation in it, be unveiled, although forever receding, asymptotically? Shall we perhaps be able to see all things, great and small, glittering with new light and reborn meaning, ancient but now again relevant in an iconic image which is related to our own time and experience?

The cosmic significance of this panorama is revealed when

we consider it as the stages of an evolution that has achieved the rise of man and his consciousness. This is the new plateau on which we now stand. It may seem obvious that the succession of changes, sustained through a thousand million years, which have transformed microscopic specks of protoplasm into the human race, has brought forth, in so doing, a higher and altogether novel kind of being, capable of compassion, wonder, beauty and truth, although each form is as precious, as sacred, as the other. The interdependence of everything with everything else in the totality of being includes a participation of nature in history and demands a participation of the universe.

The future brings us nothing, gives us nothing; it is we who in order to build it have to give it everything, our very life. But to be able to give, one has to possess; and we possess no other life, no living sap, than the treasures stored up from the past and digested, assimilated, and created afresh by us. Like all human activities, the law of growth, of evolution, of convergence draws its vigor from a tradition which does not die.

At this point, however, we must remember that the law of growth, of evolution, has both a creative and a tragic nature. This we recognize as a degenerative process, as devolution. Whether it is the growth of a human soul or the growth of a living cell or of the universe, we are confronted not only with fulfillment but with sacrifice, with increase and decrease, with enrichment and diminution. Choice and decision are necessary for growth, and each choice, each decision, excludes certain potentialities, certain potential realities. But since these unactualized realities are part of us, they possess a right and command of their own. They must avenge themselves for their exclusion from existence. They may perish and with them all the potential powers of their existence, their creativity. Or they may not perish but remain unquickened within us, repressed, lurking, ominous, swift to invade in some disguised form our life process, not as a dynamic, creative, converging power, but as a necrotic, pathological force. If the diminishing and the predatory processes comingle, atrophy and even death in every category of life ensue. But if we possess the maturity and the wisdom to accept the necessity of choice, of decision, or order and hierarchy, the inalienable right of freedom and autonomy, then, in spite of its tragedy, its exclusiveness, the law of growth endows us with greatness and a new moral decision.

Convergence is committed to the search for the deeper meanings of science, philosophy, law, morality, history, technology, in fact all the disciplines in a transdisciplinary frame of reference. This Series aims to expose the error in that form of science which creates an unreconcilable dichotomy between the observer and the participant, thereby destroying the uniqueness of each discipline by neutralizing it. For in the end we know everything but *understand nothing*, not being motivated by concern for any question. This Series further aims to examine relentlessly the ultimate premises on which work in the respective fields of knowledge rests and to break through from these into the universal principles which are the very basis of all specialist information. More concretely, there are issues which wait to be examined in relation to, for example, the philosophical and moral meanings of the models of modern physics, the question of the purely physico-chemical processes versus the postulate of the irreducibility of life in biology. For there is a basic correlation of elements in nature, of which man is a part, which cannot be separated, which compose each other, which converge, and alter each other mutually.

Certain mysteries are now known to us: the mystery, in part, of the universe and the mystery of the mind have been in a sense revealed out of the heart of darkness. Mind and matter, mind and brain, have converged; space, time, and motion are reconciled; man, consciousness, and the universe are reunited since the atom in a star is the same as the atom in man. We are homeward bound because we have accepted our convergence with the Cosmos. We have reconciled observer and participant. For at last we know that time and space are modes by which we think, but not conditions in which we live and have our being. Religion and science meld; reason and feeling merge in mutual respect for each other, nourishing each other, deepening, quickening, and enriching our experiences of the life process. We have heeded the haunting voice in the Whirlwind.

The MÖBIUS STRIP

The symbol found on the cover of each volume in Convergence is the visual image of *convergence*—the subject of this Series. It is a mathematical mystery deriving its name from Augustus Möbius, a German mathematician who lived from 1790 to 1868. The topological problem still remains unsolved mathematically.

The Möbius Strip has only one continuous surface, in contrast to a cylindrical strip, which has two surfaces—the inside and the outside. An examination will reveal that the Strip, having one continuous edge, produces *one* ring, twice the circumference of the original Strip with one half of a twist in it, which eventually *converges with itself.*

Since the middle of the last century, mathematicians have increasingly refused to accept a "solution" to a mathematical problem as "obviously true," for the "solution" often then becomes the problem. For example, it is certainly obvious that every piece of paper has two sides in the sense that an insect crawling on one side could not reach the other side without passing around an edge or boring a hole through the paper. Obvious—but false!

The Möbius Strip, in fact, presents only one monodimensional, continuous ring having no inside, no outside, no beginning, no end. Converging with itself it symbolizes the structural kinship, the intimate relationship between subject and object, matter and energy, demonstrating the error of any attempt to bifurcate the observer and participant, the universe and man, into two or more systems of reality. All, all is unity.

I am indebted to Fay Zetlin, Artist-in-Residence at Old Dominion University in Virginia, who sensed the principle of convergence, of emergent transcendence, in the analogue of the

Möbius Strip. This symbol may be said to crystallize my own continuing and expanding explorations into the unitary structure of all reality. Fay Zetlin's drawing of the Möbius Strip constitutes the visual image of this effort to emphasize the experience of coalescence.

R.N.A.

ACKNOWLEDGMENTS

This book did not come forth without much help. I wish to acknowledge my appreciation to Harper and Row for permission to use figures 1 through 5, published in my book *World Population and Human Values*. I especially want to thank Lydia Bronte, and my son Jonathan, who delved into the notebooks helping to make coherent the unedited pages of manuscript, and Jagdish Mehra for his later contributions to this process. Lorraine Friedman and Barbara Robinson, as always, sources of infinite patience, provided immeasurable assistance in transcribing my not-always-legible notes. My wife Francoise Gilot has consistently encouraged and supported my sometimes tentative desires to write and to communicate and she once again lent her wisdom and criticism. And lastly, of course, I am indebted to Ruth Nanda Anshen, without whom this book would never have seen the light of day.

Anatomy of Reality

I knew that civilization needs a religion as a matter of life or death; and as the conception of Creative Evolution developed I saw that we were at last within reach of a faith which complied with the first condition of all the religions that have ever taken hold of humanity: namely, that it must be, first and fundamentally a science of metabiology.

Of life only is there no end; and although of its million starry mansions many are empty and many still unbuilt, and though its vast domain is as yet unbearably desert, my seed shall one day fill it and master its matter to its uttermost confines. And for what may be beyond, the eyesight of Lilith is too short. It is enough that there is a beyond.

George Bernard Shaw

From *Back to Methuselah: A Metabiological Pentateuch*, World's Classics #500 (New York: Oxford University Press, 1947), pp. lxxii, 245. (The play was first published in 1922.)

INTRODUCTION

Humankind, seen as an organism, seems to be undergoing a major transformation that resembles the maturation processes of biological development—the growth of child to adult or the metamorphosis of tadpole to frog, caterpillar to butterfly. In a way, it also resembles the kind of evolutionary processes that have resulted in the emergence of new species. We are witnessing not only technological changes in our society but changes in the minds of individuals and shifts in the perceptions of the collective mind as well.

The context of our lives has altered radically; as a consequence we ourselves are being affected. The changes are both subjectively sensed and objectively observed. In my own life, I have felt impelled to explore my own perceptions of reality and to explore the way my mind works in response to these immense pressures and changes. Over the years I have developed a personal cosmogony—a way of looking at the world with the concept of evolution as a central metaphor—that has provided me with an effective basis for understanding and, at times, dealing with the myriad changes we now face. With the urging and encouragement of Ruth Nanda Anshen, I have responded to my own desires to share these insights and perceptions with others.

The original text, culled and edited from notebooks of meditations and sketches, has become this unorthodox volume. Its form is more meditative, circular, or spiraling than it is linear, and the themes are interwoven, as they are in my own mind. The quality of the text thus reflects both the nature of my own thought processes and, as I see it, the nature of the evolutionary process itself, which does not proceed in a direct path to some particular goal, but goes through many meanderings in the process of adaptation and change.

The concept of universal evolution, as described here, provides a paradigm for a more expanded view of human experience than many other models. Seeing ourselves in an evolutionary perspective reveals our relationship to all other natural phenomena. Thus, the paradigm of evolution lays the foundation for a cosmogony that includes human beings as an integral part of the cosmos.

The human mind, that increasingly complex system which imagines, reasons, creates—the initiator of culture—is the most recent, the most elaborate of the emergent evolutionary phenomena. Dynamically active, it has given us the power to split atoms, transmute elements, create new genes, and even the capacity to destroy ourselves and render our planet lifeless. It has also given us the ability to save lives threatened by disease, to prolong human life, and to create new forms of life. It is the source of art, philosophy, science, and of the ingenuity to improve the quality of life. It is the wellspring of wise choices and wise decisions. It is also the source of creations antithetical to life; it is the creator of imbalances, conflicts, cruelties, and weapons of destruction that now threaten the very existence of life. However, one of the central ideas in this book is that this creative power of the mind can be directed to guiding and to fulfilling the potential of the human race to the limits of its genetically determined endowment.

The ideas in this volume arise from my feeling that there is need for a simplified way of seeing the importance of the human mind in evolution. As human beings, we are enmeshed in the process of evolution as active, and not merely passive, participants. The emergence of the human mind has brought about our involvement by giving us a capacity to anticipate and react to our circumstances in a way unique among species. The mind makes it possible for us to reflect upon the cosmos; it may even be said to *reflect* the cosmos, a sentient mirror which gives us a way of seeing all that has gone before us in the course of existence. The human mind also enables us to imagine possibilities that might develop in the course of future evolution, and moreover to influence the direction of this process.

We thus have a profound responsibility in the continued evolution of the human species. A sense of concern and urgency about our future has been expressed by many contemporary thinkers, and the thinking that forms the basis for this volume arose largely out of that sense of responsibility. I do not write here, however, as an expert in evolution or in human life, but from the point of view of a physician-biologist, trained in science, with a special interest in evolution, and possessed of a wide range of human experience. I make no pretense of having an answer to the problems with which humankind is confronted. My purpose is to share a perspective that has been shaped in the course of my asking questions, not only in terms of my experience but in terms of our knowledge of cosmic evolution as well. Only as my horizon became enlarged to this extent did I feel that I had a useful way of understanding the human predicament.

It is too early to do more than make tentative suggestions about the meaning of what is happening in our time, or about what it may purport for the future of human evolution. We are in a period of ambiguity and uncertainty which tempts the conclusions of both pessimists and optimists. It is far too soon to know who may be right. Similarly, it is too early to see clearly what are the best choices to make and the best way to proceed in balancing ourselves between the needs of the present and the future. At this time, it seems prudent merely to draw attention to what is happening, in a way which does not take too firm a directional position, yet is based upon a recognition of the hard realities with which we are confronted.

The central theme of this volume is that, if we are informed about what is happening in our age and about options that face us, then, as individuals as well as members of the organism of humankind, we may be able to choose the most evolutionarily advantageous path. This idea is based upon the assumption that, either because of genetic determination or through intellectual/ intuitional development, a sufficient number of human beings now exist who, as individuals, are impelled to counter the self-destructive and devolutionary influences in our society and in the world.

PERCEPTION

DISCOVERY

In order to understand what follows it will be necessary for me to refer to certain effects of inverted perspective which I have found valuable in my scientific work and which I have also used as a device to understand the human condition. I do not remember exactly at what point I began to apply this way of examining my experience, but very early in my life I would imagine myself in the position of the object in which I was interested. Later, when I became a scientist, I would picture myself as a virus, or as a cancer cell, for example, and try to sense what it would be like to be either. I would also imagine myself as the immune system, and I would try to reconstruct what I would do as an immune system engaged in combating a virus or cancer cell.

When I had played through a series of such scenarios on a particular problem and had acquired new insights, I would design laboratory experiments accordingly. I soon found myself in a dialogue with nature using viruses, immune systems, and other phenomena to ask questions in the form of experiments and then waiting for the answer. Based upon the results of the experiment, I would then know what questions to ask next, until I learned what I wanted to know, or until I went as far as I could go. When I observed phenomena in the laboratory that I did not understand, I would also ask questions as if interrogating myself: "Why would I do that if I were a virus or a cancer cell, or the immune system?" Before long, this internal dialogue became second nature to me; I found that my mind worked this way all the time.

When I started to ask larger questions about the human world, it came naturally to me to play the same kind of game. I soon found myself shifting my perspective, as I did in relation to my scientific work, from that of the participating subject to that of the objective observer. When I began to look at myself and at

8 PERCEPTION

conditions of human life, I sought a perspective from outside myself and outside the "here and now," as well as from within. I needed a different, broader perspective.

Several years ago I began to use the curve of human population growth and the S-shaped sigmoid growth curve (figure 1 and figure 2) as a way of trying to understand what is happening in our time. I discovered that I could shift perspective from what I have called "here and now," to what I have named "outer time and outer space." In doing this I was able to see relationships and processes that I had not previously seen.

I realized that I had discovered a useful way to understand what was happening in the world and to examine its relationship to nature—to the evolutionary process, and to the human mind. I was able to imagine myself outside these phenomena as well as in them, in the same way as I had been able to imagine myself inside or outside a virus, or a cell, or an immune system. I began

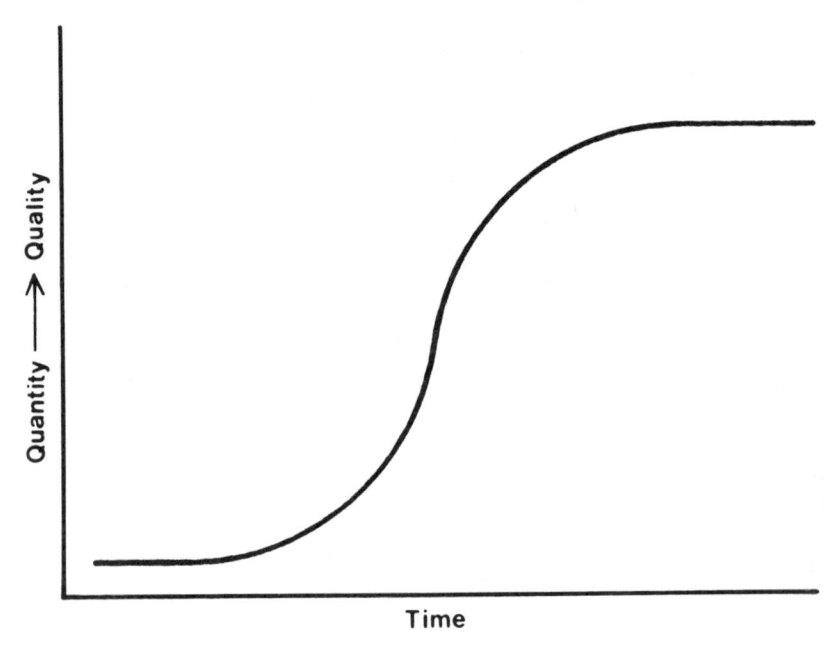

Figure 1. The evolutionary path: the S-shaped curve.

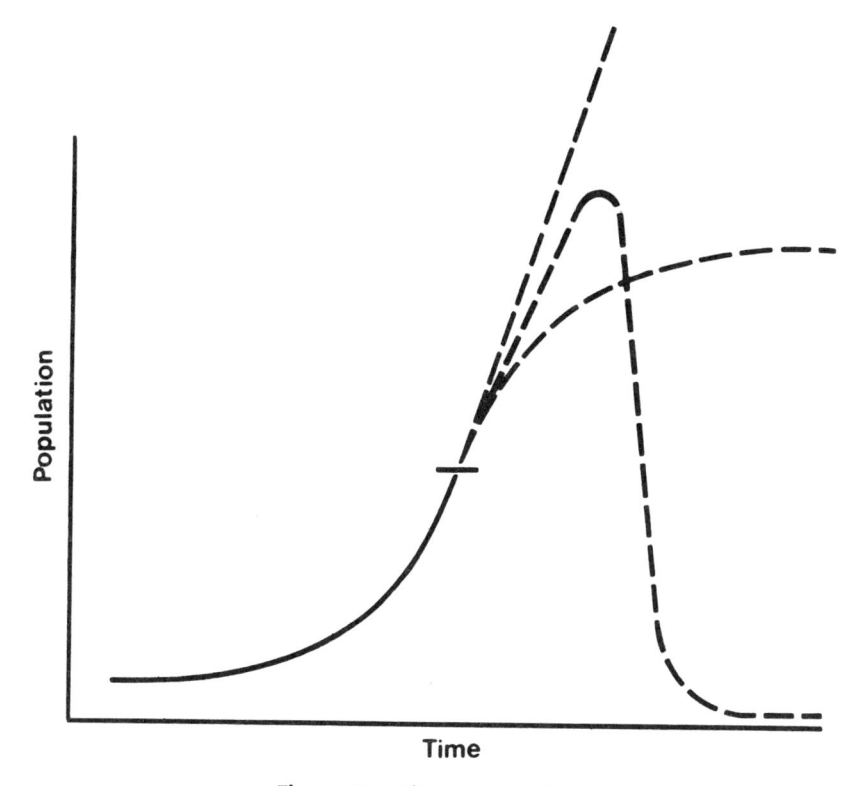

Figure 2. Alternative paths.

to imagine what might be done to ameliorate or to improve the human condition, just as I had tried to imagine what could be done to destroy the infectivity of a virus without removing its capacity to immunize; what I would do to stimulate the immune system against a disease without the organism having to go through the experience of the infection itself.

I have continued to play the same mind-game in relation to the human predicament. I was clearly aware that I was using my imagination to explore reality; I wanted to know whether I could test the subjective perceptions accumulated in this way for correspondence to empirical, or objective, reality. In the laboratory I did so by means of experimentation; in real life, I looked to life's experiences for objective evidence for or against the tentative conclusions I had reached. I soon found that this system worked as well in trying to understand human experience as it did with experiences in nature. I also found that there were powerful analogues between the two and when used together each could enrich the other interactively. In other words, the body of knowledge, or the epistemology, of science had something to offer to the epistemology of human experience, and vice versa. When this became apparent to me I was as much at home as an epistemologist of science as of human experience, and I was able to move from one domain to the other in the same way as one moves from the house in the city to the house in the country. I could work in the house of science in the city and play in the house of human experience in the country. I could be at home as an objective/subjective scientist in one state of mind and as a subjective/objective human being in another state of mind.

This experience underlined, in a very striking way, the value of being able to look at any event in life from more than one perspective. Being able to see things and to see oneself only from one point of view entailed limitations. When I had had the experience of seeing from many different points of view, I could see and feel so much more; I then discovered what the words identification and empathy meant. I could identify with a virus or a cell or with the immune system; I could also empathize with people in different situations, circumstances, and states of mind. I realized that, objectively speaking, there was not one fixed point of view or one perspective, but many changing points of view that depended upon varying circumstances. This revealed to me the value of participation as well as of suppleness and flexibility in my own perspective as an observer. I developed the capacity to shift my perspective.

In this way I could manage to solve problems more easily because I could look at the problem from the viewpoint of subject and object at one and the same time. I found myself at one with the object, or with the subject, and I could even project myself in time, through my imagination, and bring to realization intentions or imaginings as if they had become self-fulfilling prophecies. I then imagined that it may be possible, through empathy and intention, to influence the future course of human events in the same way that we can influence the course of human events through the use of the scientific and artistic imagination. I recognized the importance and value of the mind and the value of the game of empathetically shifting perspective in dealing with human problems as well as in unraveling the mysteries of nature. If the human mind can do one, it should be able to do the other.

HUMAN MIND IN EVOLUTION

My interest in viruses and cells and in the immune system arose because they are often the cause of disease and can be studied and manipulated to create remedies for treatment or prevention. In the same way, I have become interested in the human mind and in evolution, because I see them both as the cause of the human predicament and as the means for its amelioration.

Our present difficulties have arisen through the continued evolutionary development of the human mind, especially with the developments in science and technology. These have created the conditions not only for the increase in human population but also for many other contemporary changes in the quality of human life. Physically, the quality of life in the more-developed parts of the world is relatively better than it was in the past. But in terms of mental health and life styles, new sets of problems exist as a result of the changes that have taken place in recent years. Since these problems are products of the human mind, and since the human mind is a product of evolution, I see these both as closely interrelated factors contributing to the present human condition.

Just as we look into the causes of diseases for a clue as to their remedy, so we can look into the human mind and into the process of evolution itself for clues to the remedy of the maladies from which human beings are now suffering. If the causes stem from the evolutionary process itself, then what can be expected and what can be done to deal with them? If the causes lie in the human mind as a result of its evolution, then in what way is this knowledge useful as a means for solving these problems?

It is this aspect of the present predicament to which I wish to draw attention. For if my assumption as to causes is true, then it is upon evolution, including the evolution of the human mind, that we may have to rely for solutions. We may then look to natural history for clues as to what we might do to reverse negative trends and bring about a change in the collective human mind that would constructively influence the course of the human future.

The importance of this idea lies in the effect it could have upon the collective human mind in looking for the causes of our individual and collective difficulties. We are all victims of the same process, or will all soon become its victims. And we all possess within ourselves, to a greater or lesser degree, the capacity to remedy what is happening in the world today, along with the responsibility for doing so.

When we see ourselves in this way, as simultaneously the victims and as the causes of the effects we wish to correct, we change our way of thinking about ourselves and our difficulties, and we can seek more appropriate and effective remedies and preventives than if we were to imagine other, less relevant or less significant causes.

Through the capacity of my mind to identify with nature and with evolution, I imagine all kinds of things that might be considered in dealing with the precarious state of human existence. The crucial stage in which we find ourselves resembles the stage of metamorphosis seen in other living systems. It suggests that there is an evolutionary remedy to the human predicament—one that seems to be built into our genes, so to speak. We may, indeed, possess the capacity to evolve through the present stage into a higher stage of development. If, in fact, this does take place, then it will occur through the evolution of the human mind, which will provide the cure rather than remain the cause of the disease that now afflicts us.

This idea emerges from an evolutionary perspective of the human condition. It represents a more optimistic view than its opposite, which views humankind as incapable of solving its evolutionary problems—the problems of our relationship to nature, to our planet, and to each other—and therefore doomed to rapid extinction. The more optimistic view suggests that there is built into the evolutionary process the means for continued evolution as one method for survival and that we ourselves are evidence of the existence and efficacy of such a process. While more species have become extinct than have survived and evolved, human beings represent the most advanced form that has as yet emerged in the course of evolution. It remains to be seen whether the present version of human beings will render themselves extinct or whether more highly evolved human beings will emerge, capable of solving the problems that are the cause of the human predicament, and avoid extinction. Does human nature, through the evolutionary process, possess this capacity, and will human beings discover how to master this aspect of their own nature to their own advantage? If this possibility exists, and if it is acknowledged by the human mind, will it react in such a way as to move in this direction? We will know, in due course, whether or not such movement will come into evidence. In spite of the almost overwhelming evidence to the contrary, there are indications that it is occurring.

It now remains for human beings to decide, and not merely for the future to decide, the ultimate course of human evolution. By imagining ourselves inside the process of evolution and by imagining the process of evolution working inside our minds, we may discover how to deal with the problems as well as with the opportunities arising from our unique role in the natural world, and we may learn how to empathize in a way that might influence the direction of evolutionary choices. This would mean the refinement of the capacity to imagine what goes on in the human mind at all stages in its development and to discover what needs to be done to prevent its crippling, in the same way that we have discovered ways of avoiding the paralysis and crippling of limbs attributable to certain viruses. In this respect, we are now in an evolutionarily advantageous position. We have gone beyond the use of science and technology to control nature; we are now in a position to influence the healthy development of the human mind through the use of the concepts of science and scientific knowledge, applying such concepts to the study of the human mind, and using the knowledge so gained for improving the quality of the minds of humankind.

The development of sciences focused on the human mind and human behavior gives hope that this may be the direction in which we are going. Breakthroughs in knowledge in the physical and biological sciences have led to the present stage in human evolution. They have set the stage for the next breakthrough in knowledge in the human sciences. The necessity for such a development is universally felt.

When the potential for continued survival is threatened, nature and the evolutionary process appear to possess the capacity to respond. If the response does not occur soon enough, or does not take place at all, a negative effect is seen. If it does occur soon enough, a desirable adaptation ensues. These phenomena are well known in developmental biology, in evolutionary biology, in agriculture, and animal culture, and I suggest that they exist in what might be called *Homo* culture.

The scientific basis exists for knowledge, gained experientially and experimentally, to be applied to the highest development of the human mind. This will require a commitment and an involvement far greater than presently exists. However, there are signs that this commitment and involvement is now expanding. There are many more scientists now than before whose interest and curiosity have been captured by the opportunities that exist for the further development of the human mind.

As in every evolutionary process, there is a great deal that remains unknown. However, attention in this instance is more advantageous than neglect. The increasing attention being given to this important area offers encouragement for the future, and hope in the present.

THE GREAT MYSTERY

My mind is occupied by shifting patterns and changing relationships as if I were observing through my mind's eye the process of evolution and the related processes of metamorphosis. I am drawn and guided by feelings to move, to act, to observe, and to reflect on what all this means. I sense something strong and powerful that is acting with interior as well as exterior force. I feel it as I feel the wind although I cannot see it. My sail is full but I do not see what fills it. I am drawn toward certain people and in certain directions. Forces of attraction act upon me; they guide me as if I did not need a compass with which to verify my course. It is enough that I should yield and allow myself to follow what I feel.

This is mysterious. I cannot visually, with my physical eye, see the forces that act upon me from within and without and yet I cannot deny their existence. If I try, I suffer. If I surrender, allowing them to act upon me, and if I work with them, I feel exhilarated; I become filled with the joy of life.

I do not understand these forces, nor how they work. I only know of their existence by what I feel. Then I begin to think about what they might be and what they seem to be telling me. Things, people, situations appear to be right or wrong. At first, I often don't know why. Only later do I understand and see in perspective; then I recognize a pattern. What is responsible for the pattern? How is it constructed? What are the principles? What is the basis of the order and consistency of the patterns that unfold? What does it mean? What does it tell me that I must try to understand through my thoughts and feelings? What does it signify? I cannot answer these questions at once. I can only yield to the forces which act upon me and move in the direction toward which I am drawn, to a destination for which I have neither map nor compass. I have never been there before.

As it is for me, so it is also for others. I must, therefore, allow myself to be guided by the forces that act upon me. When I have found the way I shall know whether it is the right direction and whether it is the evolutionary path into the future.

I don't know what lights up my way. There must be others who help illuminate the way for me, often with lights that I can see but that are invisible to them. Perhaps this is what I, too, do for them. This may well be how the way will be illumined, how the light will be seen toward which still others will be drawn. This is the inner light that becomes the beacon, the guiding beam that projects from within a vision toward which we are drawn.

We can perhaps explain what is happening in the world today by recognizing the many different visions, the many different perceptions, the many different world views as representing the goals toward which different people are drawn. Some will pursue the evolutionary path, while others will fall from it.

It is not possible to know objectively which of the many paths to follow. However, there is a way of knowing that has led us to where we are today. We are part of a long continuity, part of a sequence of events in a continually unfolding pattern, the future of which we would like to see but cannot until we get there. And yet there must be something that guides us, something that we sense through our feelings and, guided by our reason, upon which we can rely. How can we know from among the many forces that bear upon us, from among the various impulses from within and the various pressures from without, which to choose, to which to yield, which to follow? This is when we can be as seriously misled by rationalism as by illusion. This is the great mystery that affects the human being; it is the mystery of human life, its order, its beauty, its caprice. This is also the great mystery of the disorder, the ugliness, and the blind determination of those who plunge headlong into self-destruction.

In what do we trust? How can we know in what to trust? How can we know the meaning of our reason and our intuition?

It may well be that the answers to these questions lie in reality, in testing our intuition and our reason in experimentation, in life's experiences. But how can we know what reality is? How can we discover the source of wisdom, that we may then know whether our intuition and our reason may be trusted?

We can discover that our intuition and reason are right by testing them. This kind of testing, however, can either be fatal or it can lead to great enlightenment and to the evolutionary path. Can I know which it might be by how I feel at the moment? What of the next moment? Will I know more later? Will I have a way of knowing something more certain than if I act now, if I choose now? What if the decisive moment passes? This is the great mystery. This is where intuition and reason working in harmony can help each other and can help us. This is the way to know, the way with the greatest certainty. Only the test of reality will then tell us whether we were right or wrong, whether our intuition and reason were functioning in an evolutionarily sound and effective manner. Only by cultivating and refining the processes of intuition and reason complementarily, only by reconciling them each in the service of the other, can we achieve the wisdom we seek. Only by drawing on the wisdom of nature, the source of our intuition, and using the experiences and wisdom of the human being, the source of our reason, can we begin to approximate—by feeling and by thinking—what reality will say when the experience has been attempted and completed. Only in this manner can we develop the confidence we seek in knowing how to proceed and what to do with the temptations, the options, and the choices with which we are confronted each moment of every day.

Thus the individual and humankind are intimately linked as is the part to the whole. Man is linked to the cosmos as well as to all other human beings and, in one way or another, human beings have feelings for each other whether they are remotely or closely related. Human beings have a feeling, sensitivity, and understanding for where they are in the cosmos and in the world, in time as well as in space. There are some among us who feel and see more clearly than the rest; they are the ones who illuminate and reveal reality for others. This feeling, sensitivity, and vision give us our orientation and our sense of relationship to ourselves, to others, to the world, and to the cosmos. It is this feeling and understanding that link us to our historical and evolutionary past and future. It is this understanding together with all the other human attributes, biological and metabiological, innate and acquired, that creates the possibility for human beings to influence the evolutionary process, to become either the preservers or the destroyers of the evolutionary process. It seems to me, therefore, that the battle in which we are presently engaged is between the pro- and the antievolutionary forces. The battle will be long and will be fought on many fronts.

We are at an important juncture in human evolution, and even, one might say, in cosmic evolution. The role of reason and intuition in the process of knowing, of knowing what is right and wrong in terms of what is evolutionarily right and wrong, is beginning to be perceived more than ever before. The merging of intuition and reason will provide wisdom for the resolution of the struggle in which we are engaged.

PROCESS

If I were nature, what, in the course of playing with all that I had invented, created or discovered, would I have done as I recognized the emergence of the precursors of the human mind and what would I have done when I discerned the human mind itself?

If I were evolution, operating *sui generis*, not knowing what I was doing until after it had been done, until after it had happened, and if I could then test it and choose—through natural selection—the best with which, and upon which, to build, what would be the characteristics and the properties of the mind, or the minds, that I would have found the most desirable to favor, to select, and to build with and to build upon?

As a product of this process, I am trying to put myself in evolution's place so as to learn, through the use of my imagination, what evolution might have "intended" in the course of "playing its games" of mutation, creation, and selection. Looking at evolution in this way, it seems to me that the phenomenon of survival has emerged and persisted because of its value for the perpetuation of the evolutionary process. Survival has persisted because it is necessary for continuing the process of evolution, the process of perpetual creation. At every point when a self-generating form appeared, this phenomenon was the basis for allowing it to continue on its own momentum and be tested for its ability to create or to invent new forms, new devices, and new ways of perpetuating the process of evolution. This implies that, at the point in time when the mind of man appeared and began to function as an instrument capable of autonomous creation, invention, and evolution, it became even more inventive and creative than nature and began to learn nature's strategies, nature's game, so to speak. In our present era our minds are even beginning to use nature in ways that might lead to man's own destruction and the obliteration of the human mind itself.

As this takes place, it would be wise if nature, in order to protect its own magnificent creation, would favor and select those human minds which have the capacity to correct the destructive tendency, to arrest this process and become the dominant force for the continuation of evolution for its self-perpetuation.

It seems obvious that, having gone this far in the process of evolution, nature would inevitably discover the difference between the constructive and destructive tendencies it had created—tendencies that might be called morphic and entropic. Through the course of chance events, patterns emerged that then became nature's laws, upon which and with which more complex forms and structures could be built, serving the evolutionary process. The building blocks of matter and the infinite number of their possible arrangements and relationships created more and more complex forms. One of the most complex is the genetic code, which led to more rapid and efficient evolution than in any other form of matter that had previously appeared.

The genetic code was capable of enormous variation, and with its appearance the time scale of evolution was greatly foreshortened. The genetic code itself is self-reproducing and autogenerating. Before the genetic code emerged evolution had proceeded slowly through changes in physical matter alone. When living matter appeared, it became a more rapid means for evolution to proceed. The process then continued on its own, involving the selection of the most successful and effective forms for continuing evolutionary complexity.

In time it appears as if nature's role became one of protecting and assuring the selection process and the capacity to discriminate between what was of greater evolutionary value, i.e., adaptive value, than anything that had appeared before. Nature's game seemed to be to allow those forms to evolve and survive that possessed the greatest capacity for adaptation. It now seems that evolution emerged as the ultimate adaptive response to threats to survival, the greatest threat being that of extinction.

It follows that human extinction would result from the human inability to develop an evolutionary response to the self-destructive tendency that exists within the human species itself. This would mean, according to the way in which evolution works, that it is important to select those human forms that have the capacity to react as a part of nature, and to select their pro-evolutionary rather than antievolutionary counterparts. This would mean that there now exists the human capacity to choose those forces that are for survival in cooperation with evolution, rather than those that are antisurvival or antievolutionary. This is the basis upon which the human prospects for survival and evolution depend.

The patterns that have evolved have proliferated into many diverse forms. This is evidence of nature's success in the selection of those forms, processes, and phenomena which favor continuing evolution.

Survival depends upon the capacity of human beings to learn from nature in order to develop evolutionary responses to threats to evolution's own survival. The capacity of the human mind to respond in this way constitutes the critical factor in the persistence of the human species, which may lead to forms that more fully fulfill man's evolutionary potential.

It appears that this is the crucial and critical choice with which the human species is confronted. In this respect, nature and man are not yet in accord, and it would seem that if nature had its way man would choose the course for survival and, hence, for evolution. This choice will depend upon the functioning of the human mind and even upon the shaping and orienting of the human mind to make that choice, and upon selecting those human minds that may contribute most effectively to an evolutionary path.

CONCEPTUAL MAPS

There are limits to the capacity of the mind to examine and experience itself. I begin with the recognition that we are limited by the intuitive and reasoning capacities of the human mind and by our respective abilities to probe the limits to which we can understand the human mind and the cosmos. Nevertheless, and in spite of the absence of any hope for agreement, we can still utilize our knowledge and experience by allowing intuition and reason to work upon an initial hypothesis that can then be tested for validity and usefulness. However, a single hypothesis will not be sufficient. Many different hypotheses will be needed and will evoke many more.

It does not matter with which one begins, since the process of constructing a hypothesis, and the process of selection based upon an intuitive sense of order and upon reasoning, serve as the basis for categorizing differences showing how the mind works in its patterns of intuition and of reasoning. We can start from any point in time and from any point of view. From any beginning we can then move and change our point of view by exploring the mind or exploring the cosmos. We can look at the past, the present, or anticipate the future. We can look into atoms, cells, minds, and the cosmos. There are no limits to what we can try to do but we will encounter limits to what we can achieve.

We can begin this process by constructing a frame of reference and then adding elements to it so that pictures emerge showing the relationship of the human mind to the cosmos, and to evolution. By the use of frames of reference and pictures it will be possible to define more precisely what is meant by a particular mental construct or by a given word. Thus the mind, by intuition and reason, can react to what it produces so as to modify and change the product, which in turn causes further reactions upon intuition and reason, upon aesthetic and intellectual responses.

24 **PERCEPTION**

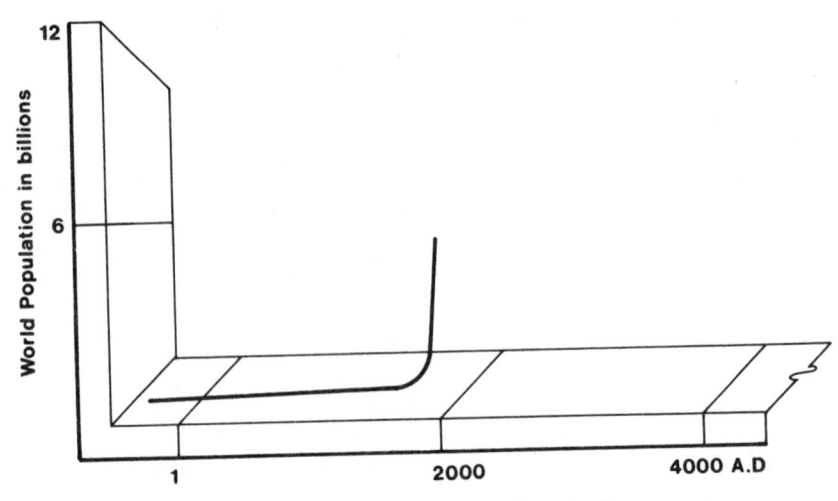

Figure 3. World population growth up to the present.

By this means it becomes possible to communicate and examine an idea or a perception intuitively and by reasoning, and even to test it by experience or by experiment. In this way a theory may be developed and subjected to verification or falsification. In this way a picture or mental construct may be approximated which attains more acceptance as it proves to be useful and

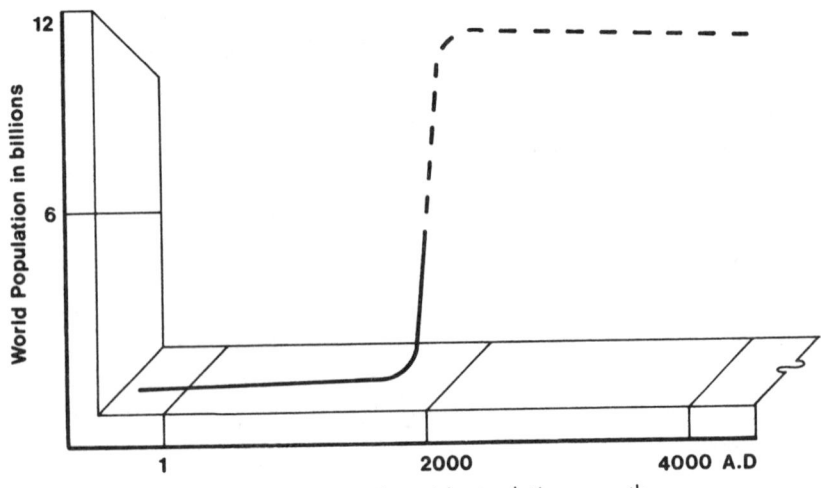

Figure 4. Projected world population growth.

advantageous in thinking about evolution and survival. The best way to illustrate this process is through example.

Let us begin with the present size of the human population and its growth in the past two thousand years (figure 3). The size of the human population is now approximately 4.5 billion. A reasonable projection over the next century and a further projection over the same period into the future suggests that a level of about 11 billion will be reached, after which a plateau will be maintained (figure 4) unless or until a major catastrophe occurs, or sources of energy and other resources for human life are depleted, rendering the ecosystem uninhabitable. The death of the sun, our prime source of energy, estimated at 3 to 5 billion years in the future, is not an imminent threat to human life. The greater and more immediate threat is less from the cosmos than from the activity of the human mind itself. Support for this view comes from figure 5, which depicts the rate of population growth over the same period and reveals the explosive increase in the human population over the past century and a half. This is happening in our time and profoundly influences the context of our lives. Our age is different in this respect from any other corresponding periods in history and will appear to

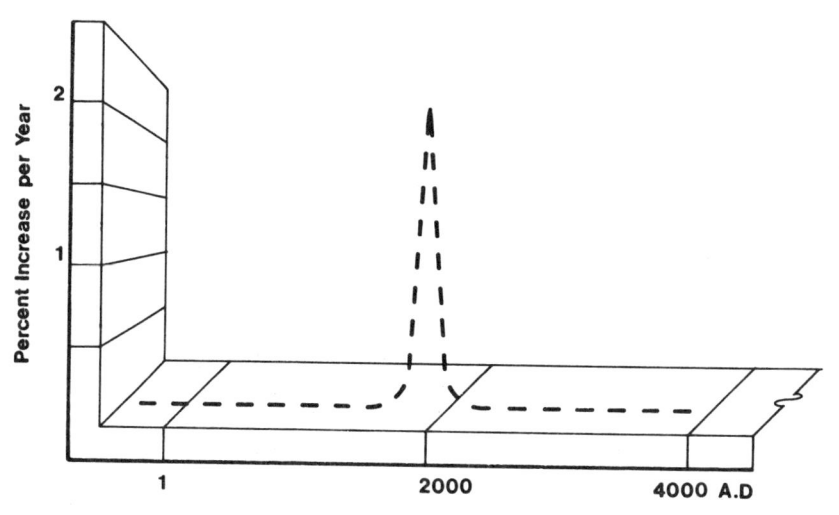

Figure 5. Projected rate of world population increase.

have been a unique episode even when viewed from some distant time in the future.

It may be said that this phenomenal increase in the human population has been caused by the processes of evolution and by the evolution of the human mind. Thus it may be seen as a natural phenomenon. If it is an evolutionary phenomenon, then what are its implications for the future? What does it suggest about all that has gone before?

Before attempting to answer this question, even in the simplest manner, I should like to offer another diagram as a more extended frame of reference so as to reveal whence we have come. If we assume that we are part of a continuum that began with the emergence of the cosmos and that we have emerged in the course of the process of evolution which originated at that time, then we can construct a diagram like that seen in figure 6. This

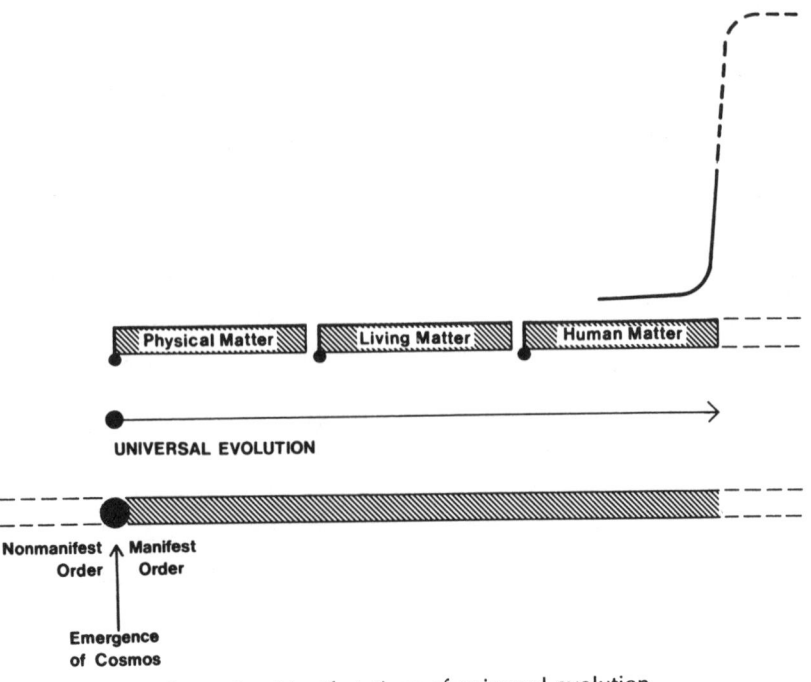

Figure 6. Manifestations of universal evolution.

illustrates the occurrence of a succession of events from a point when the cosmos appeared and evolution began.

I use the term *evolution* here in the sense of universal evolution, or evolution of the universe, and not in the restricted sense of biological evolution. The period of time when biological evolution appeared was preceded by a much longer period of prebiological evolution. In the course of biological evolution, organisms of increasing degrees of complexity emerged. In this process, the early primates appeared, leading the way to more endowed descendants: first *Homo erectus*, then *Homo habilis*, and ultimately to the recent blossoming of the human mind in *Homo sapiens*. Once the human mind appeared, metabiological evolution—evolution in the mental, cultural, creative and moral realms—became manifest. From an evolutionary point of view the differences in these three periods of time may be seen as reflecting different rates of change as well as different processes and different strategies in the process of evolution itself.

Thus, it seems that the process of evolution itself has undergone evolution. For example, the essential mechanism in biological evolution may be said to be genetic. However, in prebiological evolution subatomic, atomic, and molecular mechanisms were involved. In metabiological evolution, the period in which the human mind and human consciousness are operative, a mechanism beyond the molecular and the genetic seems to be inherent.

From figures 3–6 it would seem as if we have not yet experienced the full potential of metabiological evolution. We are an organism that has not yet been tested for adaptation to the new conditions and circumstances which have come into existence for the human species, to which we have and are continuing to contribute. The sense of urgency and the feeling of crisis to which contemporary thought is responding is related to an uncertainty of our time, part of which is evoked by the possibility that human beings may not be suited for the changes in conditions and circumstances of life suddenly imposed by a greatly accelerated rate of metabiological evolution.

From the pictures here presented, and the implications of the ingenuity that has brought us to the present stage of biological and metabiological evolution, the question arises as to whether or not we possess the capacity to adapt ourselves to the degree of "success" that has thus far been achieved as reflected in the size and the complexity of the human population.

The answer to this question lies in the prospects for the human mind to comprehend and to deal with itself and with the context of our lives. Human beings are seen as having emerged in the course of cosmic, or universal, and of biological evolution, and therefore are seen as part of a continuum in relationship to all else that exists and to all that has existed in the past since the emergence of the cosmos and in the course of its evolution.

This brief sketch is intended to suggest that evolution became manifest with the appearance of order out of nonmanifest order. When order became manifest with the formation of elementary forms of matter, it had emerged from a state of nonmanifest order in which all that has emerged in the course of evolution, including the human mind and human consciousness, was implicit.

This distillation is intended to suggest the connectedness and relatedness of all the innumerable forms in which order is contained and is manifest, including all the many phenomena in the universe and their relationship to universal evolution. Thus, universal evolution is seen as process, as flow, as a dynamic interactive development in the evolution of complexity, the most recent manifestation of which is the human mind with its capacity to reflect the cosmos and not merely to be responsive to it. The human mind possesses the capacity to develop beyond other forms in nature and has created what may be referred to as the metabiosphere (figure 7), beyond the biosphere and the physical sphere which emerged earlier in evolutionary time, and out of which human beings and the human mind arose.

Another diagram (figure 8) illustrates the growth of complexity in the universe, showing the progression from the earliest forms of order in physical matter, through living matter, and finally

CONCEPTUAL MAPS 29

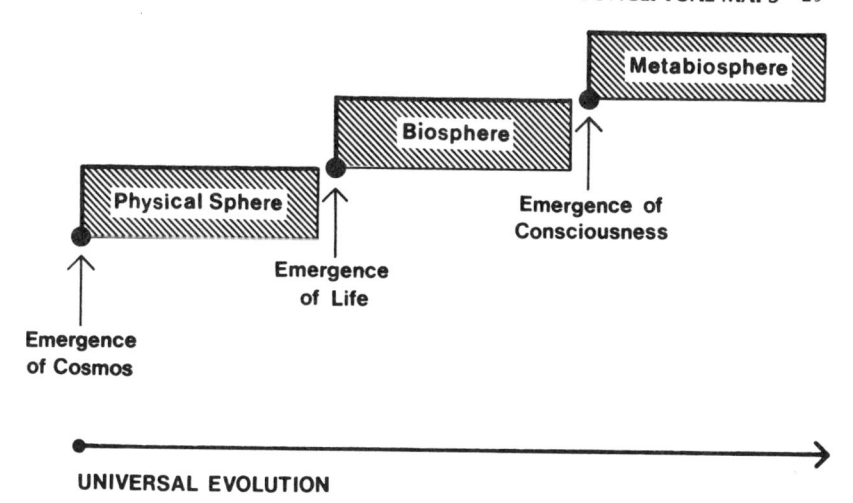

Figure 7. Evolution of manifest order.

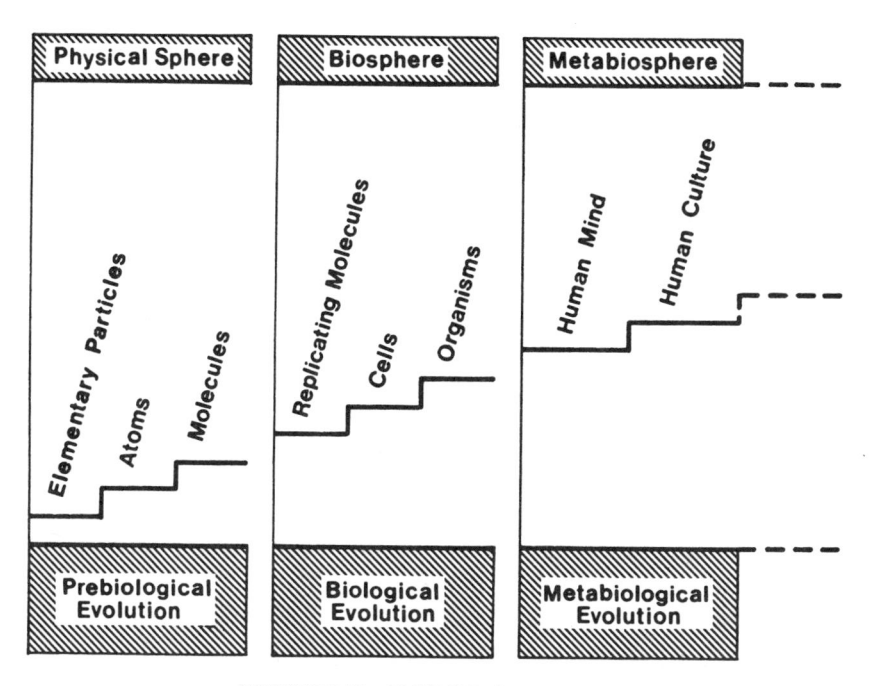

Figure 8. Evolution of complexity.

to what is referred to here as human matter. The last pertains to all that is related to the human mind itself and its creations. In the course of universal evolution, the biosphere emerged from the physical sphere and, later, the metabiosphere from the biosphere.

These distinctions, though a manifestation of the human mind, are also reflections of the many aspects of nature that have unfolded in the course of cosmic evolution. They are convenient ways of seeing differences. They reveal the relationship of the various parts to the whole of cosmic evolution, for the parts emerged in a process of unfolding of a potential that is implicit both in nonmanifest as well as in manifest order. All that preceded made possible that which came later, and all that followed was implicit in that which preceded. Thus, explicit forms existed in an implicit form before their appearance and required appropriate conditions and circumstances for their actualization.

It seems as if a basic anatomy of order must exist, as suggested in figure 9. The point in this diagram is to show the binary structure of the units at each level of complexity, suggesting that a basic anatomy or pattern exists in all systems of order—nonmanifest as well as manifest, implicit as well as explicit—a basic anatomy that exists and is manifest in each form and in all of the phenomena that have emerged in the course of cosmic, or universal, evolution. I see evolution as the process by which order unfolds in the many categories of nature. Figure 9 also proposes, in diagrammatic form, an arrangement of the disciplines concerned with order, nature, and mind, and their relation to the phenomenon of evolution itself. This figure shows the relationship of the various disciplines that have emerged in the course of metabiological development, all of which are linked, as suggested in the diagram.

At each level of complexity, the units appear to consist of two factors in a binary relationship; the double aspects of this binary structure are integrally related. They cannot be separated without dissolution of that unit, or of that level of complexity. This

CONCEPTUAL MAPS 31

UNIT	BINARY COMPONENTS	DISCIPLINE
Collective Mind	Culture / Society	Sociometabiology
Mind	Intuition / Reason	Metabiology
Organism	Species / Individual	Sociobiology
Cell	Gene / Soma	Biology
Atom	Nucleus / Electrons	Chemistry
Particle	Energy / Mass	Physics
Form	Continuous / Discrete	Mathematics
Order	Non-Manifest / Manifest	Ontology

(UNIVERSAL EVOLUTION ↑)

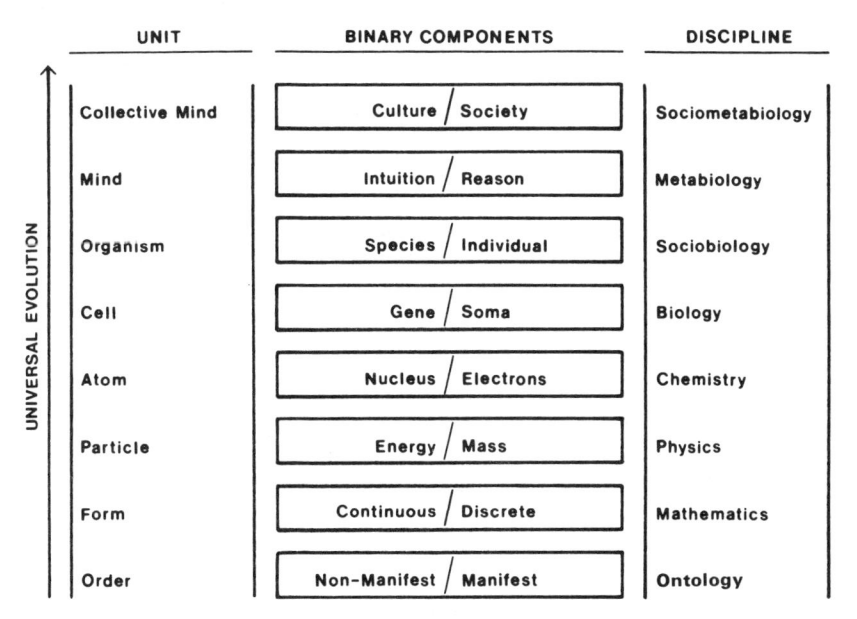

Figure 9. Anatomy of order.

diagram, which may be regarded as a conceptual map, shows the disciplines as well as the phenomena and the structures with which each is concerned. The disciplines that are concerned with nonphysical order include mathematics as well as ontology, religion, philosophy, and art. Other disciplines are concerned with the physical universe: physics studies the origin and nature of matter; chemistry and biology are concerned with the origin and nature of life; sociobiology explores the conditions of the survival of the individual and the species. Metabiology and sociometabiology examine human creativity and human culture.

Figure 10 reveals the fundamental units in the three phases of universal evolution as atom, cell, and mind, and also their binary components—nucleus/electrons, gene/soma, and intuition/reason. It also indicates the critical determinants of change as probability, necessity, and choice, respectively. The corresponding attributes, through which evolution at

PERCEPTION

UNIVERSAL EVOLUTION

	PREBIOLOGICAL EVOLUTION	BIOLOGICAL EVOLUTION	METABIOLOGICAL EVOLUTION
EMERGENCE	MATTER	LIFE	CONSCIOUSNESS
UNIT	ATOM	CELL	MIND
COMPONENTS	NUCLEUS / ELECTRONS	GENE / SOMA	INTUITION / REASON
ATTRIBUTES	INTERACTION	PROCREATION	CREATIVITY
DETERMINANTS	PROBABILITY	NECESSITY	CHOICE

Figure 10. Matrix of fundamental evolutionary relationships.

each stage is perpetuated, are interaction, procreation, and creativity. The figure suggests that whatever existed at a previous phase of evolutionary complexity was incorporated into the next higher level and whatever emerged later was implicit in previously existing forms.

The diagrams are presented at this point to introduce the concepts and relationships of the ideas embodied in them. These concepts will be elaborated and expanded in the sections which follow.

NATURE

MATTER

Nature existed for an unknowable time before the appearance of human life on earth. When we think about this, we begin to speculate about how it might have occurred. When we wonder how all this came about and why, and puzzle over the meaning of it all, including our own being, we are using our minds. The asking of questions, the imagining of possible answers, is something that is also achieved through the human mind.

We have the illusion that we do this by ourselves, in the sense that we *will* what we do and that if we would *will* to do otherwise, we could do so. When we think this way we are using our mind, which had previously come into existence without our participation. We did not *will* our having come into existence nor did we determine how we were made. Since we were not there at the beginning, nor even later along the way, and did not come onto the scene until relatively recently, we cannot know from first-hand experience. We can speculate, or theorize, but we can never have direct experience; we cannot go back to the beginning.

It is remarkable that the human mind possesses the capacity to think and to explore in these ways. Its existence is as difficult to comprehend as the existence of the cosmos itself. As we explore these questions we arrive at the edge of a precipice of understanding beyond which we cannot go without constructing hypotheses which may satisfy our need to understand. However, others may see things differently, or have different illusions, hypotheses, or theories. Some believe that an intentional God created all that exists and that human beings were separately and specially created; others say that Man created God in his own image. When we offer anthropo-morphic explanations of natural phenomena, are these projections of the human mind upon Nature or are they reflections of nature in the human mind? In the following pages I offer some of my imaginings and thoughts about nature.

In referring to nature, I include all matter that exists in the cosmos: physical, biological, and human. I imagine that before the emergence of the cosmos, before the appearance of matter in any form, something existed in an unfamiliar form. At some point it began to take the form of "primordial" matter. Scientific theories about such types of matter are the concern of physicists and astrophysicists. Through the creativity of the human mind and the study of matter, the laws of the relationship of mass and energy have been discovered, as well as the laws that govern still other phenomena that have appeared over evolutionary time. Matter and these laws must have preexisted in an implicit nonmanifest form, becoming explicit in the course of evolution. As evolution proceeded, new laws and new forms emerged. This is the way ordered complexity emerged from simpler forms.

When I try to imagine how all of this may have started, I envision what I call pure energy in a state from which matter could emerge; out of this shimmering web of energy a few specks coalesced in an orderly arrangement. The potential for this must have existed in a nonmanifest form and have been expressed through a concatenation of events. This could have happened in a number of places and even at different times, and may still be occurring in the cosmos. Once a mass of matter in any form appeared, with the force of attraction it created, the law of gravitation became evident.

It is imaginable, therefore, that larger and larger clusters of matter were formed through the force of attraction created by gravitation and culminated in one huge mass, the center of which was then put under such great pressure by the magnitude of the force generated that an explosion occurred. The resulting "big bang," which has been suggested by some scientists as the birth of the universe, was then followed by the continuing evolution of physical matter. From this primordial universe emerged the solar system and the earth. As the earth cooled, molecules with the capacity for self-replication evolved from the primitive ocean's chemical broth. Over time these became organized into cells and then into more complex organisms. Such living matter evolved at a much more rapid rate than did physical matter.

In the course of evolution in living organisms, human forms appeared, and with them the development of the human mind. With the advent of man came the capacity to create new forms that would not otherwise exist. The rate of evolution of the human capacity to create has altered the rate of evolution in a staggering way. In terms of cosmic time, the enormous changes brought about by the human mind have happened in a split second, if the time since the birth of the cosmos were compressed into a single day.

Simple rules must exist by which the cosmos is held together and functions, and all these rules are now being explored. It appears to me that the fundamental unifying principle in the cosmos is relationship. This may account for the trend toward increasingly complex relationships in all forms of matter, and even the importance for close and harmonious relationships among human beings. Relationships or kinships are needed for the orderly functioning of the human mind and seem to be inherent in the individual mind.

Kinship is fundamental as a way of relating all things to each other. It serves as a basic framework for perceiving the universe and is a way of reconciling beliefs and knowledge and of understanding their relationship.

Looking at things in this way, using the discoveries of science, reveals not only the nature of matter but the anatomy of order on the basis of which all matter is constructed. Matter at each level of complexity appears to consist of two interdependent, nonidentical elements in dynamic interaction and in integral relation to each other. It appears that an interacting, dynamic, asymmetrical binary relationship is the fundamental module of order in the cosmos. The word *cosmos* implies the existence of metaphysical (nonmanifest) as well as physical (manifest) order.

We need to probe further into the inherent logic in the universe, as well as in the human mind, to observe how these have unfolded and are revealed in and by the human mind, which reflects and is a reflector of the cosmos. One image I have is that of the cosmos as but one element in a dynamic, asymmetrical binary system, the other element of which is randomness; at the interface between the two, matter is constantly coming into and going out of the two realms of reality.

It appears that *all* units of reality are comprised of two basic elements in an asymmetrical binary relationship in dynamic interaction. A series of reciprocating causes and effects also exists. Causes induce effects which, in turn, become causes of other effects in an endless sequence leading to the complexity seen in the universe, including human evolution. This basic pattern of interactive, dynamic, asymmetrical binary relationship must exist at the metabiological and the sociometabiological levels of organization, as well as in biological and physical systems. However, it is not possible to predict, from simpler systems, the nature, or the characteristics, of the more complex systems that were to follow.

If the basic pattern of the cosmos consists of two elements integrally related, two interacting elements in close and intimate communication, i.e., functionally united, then we can expect the anatomy of the mind to be patterned after the basic structural unit at other levels of complexity in the cosmos. Complexity must have begun with the tendency toward complementary pairing. It then proceeded toward the pairing of minds, the pairing of asymmetrical elements to establish balance. This simple pattern of order is reflected in everything that exists, and is constantly active, at times achieving and maintaining dynamic equilibrium, at other times devolving and remaining unactualized. This is seen macrocosmically, as well as microcosmically.

ANATOMY OF MATTER

As noted above, one of the basic ideas that underlies my thinking, one of the images I have in mind when I contemplate the universe, is that it is constructed upon a simple pattern of order that may be seen in any and all phenomena, no matter how complex. The simple pattern is that of a binary relationship, recognized in a binary system.

The implication here is that everything in nature, everything in the universe, is composed of networks of two elements, or two parts in functional relationship to each other. This can be seen in natural phenomena as well as in human phenomena, especially when the two elements of the binary relationship are functioning in an orderly way. It is seen in functional disorder when the two elements are disturbed or disrupted. Examples may be found, in all living and human phenomena, although they are often obscured by complexity arising from the growth and development of binary relationships of increasingly higher orders of complexity. The simple pattern may be observed in great variety even in the most complex phenomena referred to in figure 9.

One example is that of a cell, in which there are two basic, essential elements upon which the existence of the unit depends and without either of which the unit would not exist: the genetic and the somatic. Though each of the two is itself complex, the simple binary pattern can be seen in the relationship between the genetic material and the rest of the constituents of a cell.

Without going into the question of the origin of the cell, or the origin of life, it is evident that the cell is a system, an essential part of which is the genetic material containing the code of information which when decoded results in the construction and functioning of the entire cell, including the genetic material itself with its capacity for self-replication. The complexity of this process is clear; nevertheless, the simple binary pattern is still evident in that the cell depends on the integrity of both the genetic system and the somatic system, each of which depends upon the existence and the healthy functioning of the other.

It becomes apparent that the genetic and somatic materials are jointly responsible for the formation and functioning of all of the cellular constituents. Some of these are responsible for constructing the genetic material itself and giving rise to the processes involved in self-replication of the genetic material and of the cell. The important point here is the independent and yet interdependent relationship of genetic and somatic material. This is made evident in "genetic engineering," by which genes can be isolated and placed in another context requiring from the latter the cellular "machinery" for the gene to function. We see, in this example, the fundamental requirement of a binary relationship for the function of a gene.

Thus, the basic unit of life, the cell, is a binary system made up of two independent, yet interdependent, elements that exist in a binary relationship for the function of the particular gene. This relationship may be characterized as *appositional* in that the two parts function together for expressing the property of the gene. There also exist in cells *oppositional* relationships in which agents act to inhibit the expression of a gene until required. Such relationships are part of the complex function of a cell, which is carried out by elements responsible for turning on or off expression or suppression, according to need, in a system of order which developed in the course of evolution.

Another example of the binary pattern is the interrelationship between the individual and the species. It is evident that a species would not exist without individuals and that all individuals are members or parts of a species. These are examples of the phenomenon of the relationship of the parts to the whole. The interrelated whole possesses properties that would not exist if the elements were not in a functional relationship to each other. The simplest such relationship is binary, as seen in pairing in living systems generally and, also, as seen in human systems. The pairing of male and female, of man and woman, as seen in biological and in human systems, is another expression of this same phenomenon. These are pairs of nonidentical or of asymmetrical elements which exist in dynamic interaction, as in all other functional binary relationships in the universe.

If this is the basic anatomical unit—the basic pattern in nature and in the universe—then relationships in living systems and in human systems can be better comprehended than if only the degrees of complexity, which are attributable to the great diversity that has developed in the course of evolution, are seen.

Evolution itself may be viewed as requiring two elements, mutation and selection, the significance of each of which is evident when functionally related. Mutations occur by chance, and selection occurs in response to necessity for survival and for continued evolution. The binary relationship of the two elements of the evolutionary process suggests that this, too, may be an expression of the binary nature of phenomena in the universe. The same may be said about the human mind in the functional relationship that appears to exist between intuition and reason.

These illustrations are intended to suggest the universality of the binary relationship, of the asymmetric binary pattern in all of the interactive dynamic relationships in nature, in physical matter (energy/mass, nucleus/electrons), in living matter (gene/soma, individuals/species), and in human matter, or the human mind (essence/existence, intuition/reason). The human mind is of an order of complexity that appeared in the course of evolution, in which matter may be said to have become conscious of itself. The phenomenon of consciousness and self-consciousness, as well as of intuition and reason, manifests the same pattern of a functional binary relationship which characterizes all matter, and all natural phenomena, from the simplest to the most complex.

DYNAMIC ASYMMETRY

My mind leaps from one set of thoughts to another as if looking for parallelisms and similarities, connections and relationships, in an attempt to understand what is happening in the world of people as well as other phenomena that I have been observing. There must be a way of seeing how all these relate to each other, to see the nature of order, the implicit order on the basis of which things are built and function. I see things differently, with more meaning, as I look for the dynamic asymmetrical binary relationship that is reflected in all the phenomena that leap into and out of my field of perception.

I have the impression that the interactions in these dynamic asymmetrical binary systems underlie all phenomena in nature. Novelty is created by such interactions, which occur by chance and are then perpetuated by the attractive (magnetic or gravitational) forces created during the growth, or increase in quality, of such pairing, and by the results of such pairing. Thus something new coming into existence in this way has a tendency to enlarge, or diminish, depending upon whether its effect proves to be evolutionary, devolutionary, or antievolutionary.

It may be easier to gain insight into the functioning of this process by examining human systems, since this process proceeds more rapidly in human systems than in other living systems. For example, the rate of evolution in the metabiosphere at present is greater than ever before. It will soon be possible to judge the characteristics of those phenomena and of those processes that have evolutionary and survival value. The use of human systems for gaining insight into the processes of evolution and into the principles underlying this natural phenomenon is the equivalent of utilizing more rapidly growing systems of microorganisms or cells for the study of genetics and of other phenomena of life at the molecular level to elucidate the details of the otherwise impenetrable process of evolution.

The rapidity with which the human mind works in its movement from one thought to another suggests the importance of thinking before an action is taken. The capacity of the human mind, in sleep as in wakefulness, when in a state to allow the binary system of the subconscious and the conscious mind to collaborate, is probably one of the most important processes involved in metabiological evolution. It may well underlie the phenomenon of creativity and may well be based upon what has been called bisociation, a process whereby pairing occurs.

This concept of pairing manifests itself in dynamic asymmetrical binary systems and their internal and external interactions. It may well define the characteristics of all living systems which have in common a similar basic functional pattern, i.e., an interacting, dynamic, asymmetrical binary plan. This suggests that this pattern must also exist in other natural phenomena. It then becomes possible to recognize the underlying unity in all the diversity of the phenomena of life, i.e., in biological and metabiological phenomena, in the biosphere and the metabiosphere. It would be of interest to study the elements of each of the binary systems, how they work separately and how they interact dynamically.

It should then be possible to isolate examples of such phenomena as models and to study them in detail so as to establish the principles and the nature of the forces involved and to note whether parallels exist in other, more complex systems. This can be done with molecular systems, or molecular events in living systems, and also with events in the metabiological realm.

RELATIONSHIP

The most fundamental phenomenon in the universe is relationship. It exists in everything. It is found in disorder as well as in order. It is in chaos as well as in cosmos. It occurs in time as well as in space. We know who and where we are, we stay in touch with our innermost selves and with the tapestry of daily life through relationships. In order to understand anything we must have a sense of the fundamental connections which form the backdrop of all experience.

The process of evolution itself is one which depends on the dynamics of relationships. Until relationships change we take them for granted; as long as a relationship is constant and stable, we assume that that is the way things are. Only when something changes do we notice. In most situations, resistance to change and the occurrence of change exist simultaneously. At moments of maximum change there is also maximum resistance to it. When relationships change it is not possible to know what will happen next, unless what is occurring has previously occurred and the outcome can therefore be predicted on the basis of prior experience. But what if something had not previously occurred? This seems to characterize the present state of affairs as far as the human predicament is concerned. It is filled with uncertainty and, therefore, with great anxiety. It tells us that we are extremely sensitive to change, to the rate of change, and that we may have reached the limit of our tolerance. We will either discover an appropriate response or we will be unable to tolerate the reality and will be destroyed.

As I write these thoughts I begin to identify myself with the phenomenon of change in the universe as well as in myself, and especially with the experience of relationship, of changing relationships, and I begin to see and to understand something about the experience of evolution from this point of view. Evolution has proceeded along the course of optimizing relationships. With respect to living things this concerns relationships in space and time, as well as relationships to the sources that furnish the necessities of life. It includes everything, internal as well as external, essential for the maintenance of the integrity and the existence of the organism, of its parts in relation to each other and in relation to the whole.

It is not difficult to see that, in the course of evolutionary time, through a long history of trial and error, patterns emerged that were particularly effective; long-lasting configurations were established thereby and the laws of nature emerged. Seen in this way, the laws of nature define the characteristics of a dynamic order, a basis upon which other forms of order rest. Even the process of evolution depends upon the existence of certain laws of order. The same is true of the human mind. Ultimately, order is recognized as different from disorder, and, therefore, one can be distinguished from the other. It is as if a sense of relationship is essential for a sense of order. The characteristics of whatever exists, including the characteristics of our lives, are based upon the existence, in one form or another, of a sense of relationship. The highest and most complex sense of relationship is expressed in consciousness. Thus, the most highly evolved form of existence is seen in the human mind, in human consciousness. It is expressed in its highest form in those who are the most enlightened and the most developed with respect to their awareness of themselves and with respect to their relationship with all else in the cosmos, near and far. Those most highly evolved would also have the greatest capacity for evolution, for advantageous change, for adaptation to changing circumstances. They would be the ones with the greatest capacity to resolve difficulties, to find ways to survive even under intolerable circumstances.

This digression reflects the way the process of evolution proceeds and also how the mind works. It also reflects what is observed in nature, the resourcefulness of nature and of the evolutionary process in the perpetuation and proliferation of order in a wide variety of forms, all of which must have a relationship to a basic pattern.

We will come to regard this as the basic pattern of order, but first I would like to establish the idea of the fundamental nature of relationship. Without relationship, order could not exist, and before order was established both order and relationship were implicit but not yet manifest. The process of evolution, which began with the emergence of relationship and of order, has been a continuation, as if in perpetuity, of the creation of new and changing relationships either spontaneously or in response to changes induced, impressed, or imposed from without.

It follows from all this that relationship is a fundamental concept as well as a fundamental phenomenon both in the cosmos and in our own lives. It is so fundamental that it may be seen as the fifth dimension in the sense that it serves to bring together three-dimensional space and the dimension of time into a whole and to provide a measure of the relationship of the parts to the whole. Thus, relationship refers to the whole of which the parts are composed, and for this reason it is to be considered as a fifth dimension.

If this is so, then we can understand the reason for the importance of relationship in our lives as well as in the cosmos, in our everyday existence as well as in the constellations in space. We see a binary relationship between energy and mass. We also see binary relationships between the elements that seem to characterize each level of complexity in nature that has emerged in the course of the process of evolution. All of these are mirrored in the human mind. The human mind appears as a reflection of the cosmos since it contains within itself the memory of, or the capacity to imagine, to recall, and to recognize, all that preceded it in the orderly process of evolution as it emerged out of disorder. It is as if evolution itself, its persistence, is a survival mechanism. It is a way by which it survives and perpetuates itself. It is as if the principal preoccupation of evolution is its own perpetuation.

If the human mind possesses the potential that exists in evolution for its self-perpetuation, then we will note in mind-phenomena tendencies seen in nature but in a form modified for the particular system of relationships that exists in and for the human mind. Thus it seems as if the phenomenon of evolution in nature and the autogenous dynamics of the human mind are in the process of convergence; when the two have become one, then the human mind will have achieved the capacity to act as evolution acts, in its capacity for adaptation to future as well as present circumstances.

It would seem, therefore, that the unifying principle of relationship is of fundamental importance and that the unity of evolution and the human mind is of special importance. That pairing is the critical convergence that we now experience, the result of which could be the next higher level in the evolution of the human mind. of consciousness, and, therefore, of the human being.

CONTEXT AND SUBSTANCE

The most significant change that is taking place today is in the context and therefore the substance of our lives. The meaning of this is difficult to appreciate. In order to do so we have to be able to see what is happening in the context and our place in it. Context is more than the physical environment. It constitutes all that exists in our relationship to space and time.

We can appreciate this when we realize how many more people exist on the face of the earth today as compared to any previous time in human history. We can also appreciate this when we recognize the rapidity with which the population has been increasing and continues to increase. This means that the rate of change, in terms of the number of people added in a given period of time, is greater than ever before. When we combine this with what has been added to the context and substance of our lives through advances in science and technology, including increases in knowledge and in means of communication, we begin to appreciate the significance of the quantitative and qualitative changes that are taking place in all of our relationships and in ourselves as well. Moreover, the change that is occurring is irreversible, as is any evolutionary change.

In order to understand these evolutionary substantive changes in terms of our individual lives, it will be necessary to appreciate what we feel as well as what we think. We can do so by recognizing what is taking place not only in ourselves but also in the world around us and in our relationships. Not only do we see the external changes but we feel their effects. They so affect our feelings as to make us wonder what is occurring. I can best describe these feelings not only in terms of space, the space in which we live, which has become increasingly overrun with people and with objects, and in terms of time, with more events taking place in shorter and shorter periods, but also in terms of the "inner space" in which we live, our mind-space, in which we experience our being. Thus we can recognize that what is happening *around* us is also reflected in what is happening *within* us. This is having an effect on our external and internal space–time relationships. It is as if the change in the context of our outer lives is also reflected in the substance of our minds. These changes affect not only our relationships but our behavior.

It would seem from this description that we may well be reaching a critical phase in which we are being tested for our capacity to adapt ourselves to such changes in relationship. This begins to awaken us to the realization of the importance of our relationship to the qualitative as well as quantitative events that are occurring.

In other living systems in which evolutionary processes operate, new forms and new structures appear when limits are reached, when new functional relationships are required for adaptation to changing circumstances. This suggests that an evolutionary perspective may explain the significance of what is taking place and may help us understand the effect these changes are having upon our minds. This also suggests the role of the human mind in this process, not only as a "victim" of the irreversible changes in context and the concomitant emergence of dangers for the future of human evolution, but also its potential role as an agent of change in affecting this process through a constructive, adaptive reaction.

The changes that are occurring in the world, and in the inner spaces of our minds, which are affected by these changes, cause us to realize the meaning of change in context, in relationship, and in substance, in terms of the whole and of the relationship of the parts to the whole. An awareness of the nature of the change that is occurring and the need to see it holistically as a profound and fundamental alteration both in reality and in our experience of this reality are essential for successful adaptation.

This is difficult to appreciate, since the changes are taking place simultaneously in us as well as around us because of our active participation in this process both as initiator and reactor. This poses special problems as we begin to accept what is taking place, and as we begin to consider ways and means to participate adaptively.

It is clear that our minds play a critical role and that the nature of our response will test our adaptability to the changing circumstances and relationships of which we have become aware. As we become conscious of the profound change in our context, substance, and relationships, and of the effects it is having upon our feelings as well as upon our behavior, we become aware of the difficulty of existing as individual human beings in an increasingly interdependent world in which competition for our minds and for our inner lives prevails. These conflicts are now so apparent as to make clear that the wars between political ideologies, as well as the conflicts between scientific and religious ideologies, are all attributable to different mind-sets, to divergent ways of perceiving and thinking. It suggests that we are required to turn our attention inward in order to deal with the problems that arise from our outer conditions.

Our inner and outer worlds are related. They do not exist separate from each other. They are two aspects of the same reality. They are two components of a mutually interactive binary relationship. The elements of each of these components, the inner and the outer, are so complex as to obscure the simplicity of this interactive relationship in which and by which evolution proceeds. It is through the process of evolution that more adequate fitness is achieved through adaptive responses which serve these goals. This appears to be a process without end and one in which universal evolution, including the evolution of the human mind will be played out with or without our participation.

EVOLUTION

UNIVERSAL EVOLUTION

The word evolution as used in this volume has a much broader connotation than when thought of in relation to the theory of evolution and natural selection as set forth by Darwin and as elaborated since the discoveries of genetic mechanisms and the relationship between genotype, phenotype, and environment. There are still many unanswered questions about the origin of different forms of life and there is continuing need for reexamining our views of evolution and of evolutionary mechanisms.

The orthodox views of evolution are presently in the process of change. The process of evolution itself is constantly evolving. We now consider evolution as both a concept and a process. This is difficult for the mind to grasp because it implies that the process of evolution and our concept of how evolution works are also evolving.

It may be easier to understand the meaning of the idea of evolution and its processes if we can accept the view that, as the process of evolution continued to emerge, it manifested itself in different ways at different rates. Just as there are different species, each of which has arisen in the course of evolution, and each of which undergoes evolutionary change, so the process of evolution itself operates differently in prebiological, biological, and metabiological systems. In metabiological processes, the rate of evolution has become more rapid than in the others. It has accelerated and its activity may be presently observed more than at any previous time in human history.

For some, the concept of evolution has assumed greater significance than the phenomenon described by Darwin and his followers. In its broadest meaning, the concept of universal evolution attempts to unify all that exists. It relates everything to a common origin and even provides a basis upon which to think of the future, as well as the present. It unites all the many branches of knowledge that have emerged in the course of metabiological development.

Since the concept of universal evolution is unifying, it possesses attributes of a principle that serves as a source of guidance. It provides a basis for a world view, and a cosmogony. It offers man a trajectory that can be identified. It suggests a way of recognizing the creation of order and purpose in the cosmos.

Cosmic or universal evolution appears to possess the self-serving purpose of retaining in perpetuity the process of evolution itself. The course of this process, which is of increasing complexity, provides the evolutionary process with the additional and more definitive purpose of becoming increasingly self-organizing and self-perpetuating. The human species and the human person serve this evolutionary process by means of the human mind and human culture.

Evolution is not linear. The form that it has taken is more like that of a tree, a complex organic molecule, an organism, or an ecosystem. Evolution has produced a wide variety of interconnected forms at all levels of organization and complexity, exhibiting similarity in one way or another, reflecting a common origin.

Evolution is a process of changing relationships. It is a process in which new relationships emerge and older relationships terminate. In the process of mutation and selection, chance plays a role. This applies as much to society and to human institutions as it does to biological systems. The forms they take are often derived from a merging of mutually useful forms and systems that previously existed.

The phenomenon of error-correction is of great advantage in the process of evolution. There must be a multitude of error-correcting mechanisms, and a hierarchy of values by which to judge error, selected over time, some more effective and of greater value than others. These are seen in complex systems with high degrees of adaptability. An imperfect system which has the capacity for correctability would be adaptable under widely diverse circumstances and would be capable of surviving and adjusting to changing circumstances.

If error-making and error-correcting are the basis for selection in the evolutionary process, then those systems that are predominantly error-correcting will be selected, and those that are inadequately error-correcting or error-preventing will not be selected. If this is one of nature's criteria for selection, we then have a basis upon which to judge qualities which we may select from among various error-reducing systems. The form of behavior selected for the qualities of performance would be judged in terms of the severity as well as of the number of errors, and serve as a basis for selection. This is self-evident in human systems. It seems also to be true in other living systems. It must also apply to the stability or dynamic equilibrium of chemical and physical systems in relation to order and function.

Different qualities are tested for fitness in the selection process. Many biological and metabiological processes, for example, are corrective for extremes through sensitive feedback effects. Success is increased by thinking ahead (feed-forward) so as to provide the basis upon which to make the best choice.

Wisdom may be a composite of foresight and preparedness based upon the existence of a repertoire of choices for a wide variety of conditions and for the availability of those which are appropriate. A system based upon mutation would provide a wide variety of choices, involving a wide diversity of possibilities. It would in all likelihood be selected in the process of evolution, and for the effective functioning of the process itself. This would require an equilibrium between stability and instability for the development of mutations and would be a reservoir of potentialities preparatory for response to changing circumstances. Oscillating systems, which serve a similar purpose, are structured essentially on the same patterns.

The systems of order that are selected, and on which all else is built, seem to be binary; the two component parts are related in such a way as to be integral to each other and then, as a unit, to become part of the next higher level of complexity.

It is necessary for every system to have internally as well as externally operating regulatory networks in order to maintain the basic structure and balance of the system. These regulatory networks also control and regulate change in a way that preserves the integrity of the system itself and even the value system upon which it is based. Value systems work in establishing the criteria on the basis of which evolutionary processes are maintained. The system is thereby maintained in a functional and healthy state.

It follows that the creation of rules to control and regulate human behavior is a necessary and natural function and is merely an extension into the metabiological realm of biological reality. However, in the metabiological realm the premise upon which laws are established, and the means for enforcing them, define the ways the minds of particular individuals and groups work, and the premises and values they espouse. Variation and diversity exist in evolution or devolution. Therefore, it is necessary to inquire into the natural attributes of a system of values and of order for evolution and survival.

Man's mind is here seen as a metasystem, a metabiological system, serving the human biological and other ecosystems in the course of serving itself. To serve itself it must preserve, and serve, other biological systems that are relevant to itself. It must, therefore, "know," intuitively and cognitively, what is of value to itself and to other systems in both the biosphere and the metabiosphere.

We can then look to the rest of nature, to the biosphere and to the physicochemical sphere, augmenting our knowledge and insights, creating and constructing a system in the metabiosphere for control and regulation that do not conflict but are in accord with the laws of nature. Such laws have evolved as part of a preexisting natural order and have been preserved and retained in the course of evolution. These natural laws must be understood and respected, and such understanding and respect must be reflected in the metabiological regulatory systems thereby preserving order in the human realm.

The human mind plays many roles; it must also regulate itself in relation to itself and to all other minds. In view of the degree of complexity implied and the individuality in development of this capacity, it is easy to understand the sense of responsibility and self-control among people, the reason for the admonitions and taboos in different cultures, including incentives for certain kinds of behavior and attitudes. Such laws would not be acceptable to all and would be broken by many for any number of reasons. It is clear, therefore, that it is necessary to exact penalties for disregarding these laws.

It is my conviction that when good triumphs over evil, it is not for moral reasons alone but as part of the evolutionary phenomenon of the error-correcting process of evolution. Although not preconceived, there appears to be a direction in evolution, an orientation toward fulfillment of an evolutionary potential such as one observes in the human realm as manifested in a discipline for performance. We can point to the existence of a sense of value, a basis for judgment, a basis for choice and selection in human beings who have the capacity explicitly to act purposefully.

In man and in nature this implies correctibility. It also suggests fallibility accompanied, however, by an openness to correction and change. We see in the world around us the existence of opposites and apposites, and the constant operation of the process of correction. This seems to be a highly developed property of all matter, in all of its multiple forms.

BIOLOGICAL AND METABIOLOGICAL EVOLUTION

Success in biological evolution is measured by adaptation and reproductive achievement. This is accomplished through strong progeny overcoming adverse conditions and competitors for the transmission of their accumulated set of genes. The gene is a unit of hereditary information that is selected for perpetuation based on the adequacy of the behavior of the organism. A number of "cooperating" genes must be involved, as well as a set of "cooperating" cell structures, for the transmission of a gene, or a trait, for survival and perpetuation.

The process of evolution may be seen as the most successful self-serving process in contriving ways by which to continue. The process of evolution itself is manifest in the different mechanisms involved in the prebiological, biological, and metabiological phases of evolution. One feature of this is the progressive increase in rate from one to the other.

Achievement in survival and evolution involves adaptation to environmental or other selective pressures which continue to shape forms that had previously overcome the adversity for gene transmission. Such pressures resulted in the selection of individuals possessing genes for adequate functioning related to the necessities for life and for self-perpetuation, i.e., for survival and for continued evolution.

In this sense genes may be looked upon as "cooperative" rather than "selfish," "obeying" the laws of the evolutionary process for maintaining itself in perpetuity. It is as if a hidden force is responsible for the behavior of the gene and of the organism, a force that for the moment I will call the force of universal evolution analogous to the force of universal gravitation. This force manifests itself in each of the different phases of universal evolution: prebiological, biological, and metabiological. A gene may be seen as a "tool" of biological evolution; it is part of a complex system for the perpetuation of order. It would seem, therefore, that achievement in biological evolution requires not only the gene that carries the information but an adequate transmission and reproductive process. This in itself requires all the complexity contained in the gene, the organism, the ecosystem, and nature, in order that it may be protected against any countervailing pressures.

Having set forth a view of the primary and subsidiary elements responsible for the evolutionary process, in all its complex variety, in the blind process of increasing order, I see similar qualities in the realm of human experience. They have in common the driving power of evolution. This includes not only the biological but also the metabiological drives. If these various manifestations of evolution coexist, they must be complementary rather than competitive, additive rather than subtractive, or substitutive. The metabiological phase is the second to appear on the scene. Even though it may seem to have dominated the first, the biological, it is still dependent upon the biological and all that has gone before it.

Only the process of evolution remains the determining factor of whatever is to persist. The evolutionary process has no regard for any species that cannot serve itself or that is incapable of evolutionary continuity. The pattern of life that has evolved favors those who respond most adequately to evolutionary requirements. This is essential for metabiological as well as for biological evolution.

The process of evolution is itself evolving, as is seen in a comparison of metabiological and biological evolutionary mechanisms. While those of metabiological evolution appear more adaptive than those of biological evolution, metabiological evolution has not yet been sufficiently tested for long-term persistence. Other experiments among species in nature have proved successful for a time but not forever, and therefore it would be of interest to examine this relatively new evolutionary process, the metabiological, in order to discern whether or not it has the capacity to correct its errors and to evolve.

In comparing metabiological and biological evolution in achieving diversity, and the criteria upon which selection depends, I would like to set forth the notion that the metabiological analogue of the biological *gene* is an *idea* generated in a person's mind. It would be analogous to a newly generated gene in a germ cell or a somatic cell. Thus, a set of ideas would be analogous to a set of genes. Since the set of genes determines the nature, character, and behavior of a cell, or of an organism, this would also be relevant for ideas. In the same way that the characteristics of an organism change, depending upon the combinations of genes that it possesses, so would the characteristics of a metabiological organism, depending upon the combination of ideas it possessed.

Thus, if metabiological mechanisms are seen as adaptive processes related to the biological, and if they have qualities of independence that could supersede the biological, then it is evident that a metabiological system could become maladaptive as well as be adaptive. If it overpowered the biological organism for which it was to provide an adaptive advantage, that organism would then have to deal with this burden, and either be destroyed by the metabiological system or discover a way to overcome its maladaptive features. Since the latter is based upon a set of ideas, it is conceivable that any that were maladaptive might change or be changed in order to restore the adaptive quality of the metabiological system if it were to better serve the human species. It may be necessary to discover ways by which we may conceive sets of ideas that would result in more adaptive attitudes and behavior.

It would follow from the foregoing that metabiological processes are not exempt from the laws of evolution nor from the process of natural selection even though they are somewhat removed from strict, direct genetic control. Since they are metabiological, they are also metagenetic and, therefore, in order to function they must possess a set of mechanisms that are analogous to other adaptive mechanisms. Thus, it is necessary to understand the way in which the adaptive quality of the metabiological may best serve the biological system to which it belongs and the methods to bring this about.

Progress and understanding occurred at a rapid rate when the biological genetic mechanism was discovered and molecular-cellular biology was born. Following that pattern, and given the evidence for metabiological evolution and the evolution of metabiological control and regulatory influences, it is necessary to approach the metabiological realm in a similar way. Hence, the search for metabiological analogues of biological phenomena.

It may well be that there are metabiological analogues of the genetic system and the immune system. As suggested above, the analogue of the genetic system would produce ideas and ideologies. The analogue of the immune system would defend them. In the human mind there is also the equivalent of "autoimmune" or autodestructive tendencies. This suggests that some of the disorders of the human mind may be dealt with by a metabiological form of "immunization," or "desensitization," or by suppressing in some way the "autoimmune" or autodestructive tendencies that arise under certain metabiological circumstances. Ideas would have to be tested just as genes are tested, or selected, for their adaptive value, or are recognized as maladaptive or neutral. It would be necessary to engage in a series of "thought experiments" to test such models, to ascertain whether or not they fit.

Darwin and Lamarck presented explanations for the origin of species, and thereby for the mechanism of biological evolution. It is clear that the Darwinian explanation better fits the facts of biological evolution, even though it may not answer all the questions concerning its nature. It seems, however, that the Lamarckian explanation, while originally proposed for biological evolution, may better fit metabiological evolution. Metabiological traits can be acquired and then passed on to succeeding generations. The genetic mechanisms described by Mendel, when combined with Darwinian ideas, do not apply directly to metabiological evolution although they do apply to biological evolution.

The challenge now is to determine in what way metabiological phenomena are adaptive or maladaptive and to ascertain the criteria for determining what is critically advantageous in metabiological systems. What, for example, is the metabiological equivalent of procreative fitness? What evolutionary purpose does the metabiological system serve? Might creativity be the analogue of procreativity, and creative capacity essential for the survival and evolution of the human person and the culture?

CREATIVITY

The answer to the preceding question lies in the idea that human creativity, like human procreativity, is necessary for the survival and evolution of the human species. It manifests itself in different forms such as in the work of scientists, artists, philosophers, statesmen, workers and craftsmen—in all those who possess the qualities of mind required for contributing creatively in their respective disciplines. These qualities are the result of many generations of evolutionary selection. This kind of metabiological evolution may be nature's way of continuing and even accelerating the process of evolution as it is a more rapid means of adaptation than occurs in biological evolution.

It is for this reason that I think of creativity as a metabiological evolutionary phenomenon. In metabiological evolution, in the way the mind works, I see parallels with the biological. I see the metabiological analogue of mutation and of the process of selection operating actively and powerfully at this point in evolutionary time.

We are utilizing our creativity to solve the problems created in the course of metabiological evolution. We have come full circle in the evolutionary spiral and need to discover the value and the meaning of this quality and of its ability to influence our perceptions. The present serious human predicament requires all our creative energies for its resolution.

Anything that affects human creativity has an influence upon the most important phenomenon on which human survival and evolution depend. The mere recognition of the significance of the phenomenon of creativity is of the greatest importance to survival and evolution and may well result in a change in the human realm by orders of magnitude, in a qualitative result that transcends any degree of quantitative change. This suggests that those events in the process of creativity that are of the greatest value cause qualitative changes in our perception, whether of a phenomenon in our experience of nature, or of the phenomenon of creativity itself. Creativity is intrinsic to the process of human or metabiological evolution. However, it is assumed, with reason, that there are self-correcting feedback effects that serve the need for continuity. If this is so, then it is possible that a new human preoccupation may be in the process of emergence, i.e., a preoccupation with human creativity. The first need is to see it as crucial for human survival and evolution. To recognize the opportunity as well as the danger implied by any ability we may have to influence, control, or use human creativity is necessary for our participation in the evolutionary process. It may well be that the greatest evolutionary advantage will lie in those who see human creativity in this light. This implies that if humankind generally were to recognize such a power in human creativity and were to develop it, the result would be an amelioration of the human condition. I cannot see any more effective way of dealing with this problem. The opportunity now exists for taking another step in human evolution, a step that involves and affects the human mind.

There are many quantitative and qualitative factors that enter into human creativity. In spite of the primary dependence upon qualitative considerations such as inspiration, emotions, and stamina, there are quantitative aspects that result in excesses and insufficiencies that have a significant effect upon creative performance. Thus, as in the playing of a musical instrument, so it is with the creative mind. The capacity to perform is inborn but training and experience are important.

There is a great deal that can still be done to improve the performance of the best minds, just as there is also a great deal that can be done to improve the performance of average minds, and even of those below average. It seems clear that the potential of the human mind in this respect can be improved by postgenetic factors. This is one of the most important functions of human society and of each individual.

However, we are so preoccupied with other matters, with individuals who are destructive, aberrant, or in some way mentally crippled or negatively creative, that we leave insufficient time for enhancing the constructive, positively creative human qualities that are needed to solve the serious problems with which we are confronted. In the face of the magnitude of our problems, we are in deep need of recognizing extraordinary human beings.

We are at a point in human evolution biologically and metabiologically at which it will be important to know how to improve the quality of the performance of the human mind, not only mentally but emotionally and physically as well. This has deep philosophical and moral, as well as scientific and technical, implications. It has implications for the art of living, the art of meaningful performance in all human endeavors. Even the art of decision making and the art of exercising choices need to be improved, just as the art of natural selection has been developed and refined in the course of evolutionary time.

It seems that when we accept ourselves as integral parts of nature, we can more easily identify with natural phenomena and learn from them what we need to know about order and disorder, the laws of nature, the nature of nature, and the nature of human nature. This is the ultimate goal in our pursuit of knowledge and the wisdom to use the knowledge we have acquired. This, now, is our great challenge.

HUMAN EXPERIENCE

The evolution of human experience occurs in the course of human experience. The evolution of knowledge takes place in the course of the increase of human knowledge. All of the many aspects of evolution depend upon one another. If the process of evolution were to cease, all human phenomena, as well as all other forms of life, would also cease to exist. The process of evolution is an essential part of all life and, therefore, cannot be separated from life, just as life and death are inseparable, are intrinsically part of each other. Without one the other could not exist.

It is necessary to understand human life in relation to the process of evolution and the process of evolution in relation to human life. In this way the role we play as products as well as instruments of the evolutionary process becomes evident and we become conscious of ourselves not only as the trustees of evolution but as agents through which the process preserves itself. The effect upon us is not perceived in precisely this way. It occurs and operates in us, with us, and upon us at an unconscious level. Relatively few are aware of what is occurring subconsciously; some are aware of influences that they perceive to be external to themselves, which they then attribute to mystical forces, such as the will of God or divine inspiration.

One way in which the phenomenon of evolution is made manifest is in human creativity. Not only is the phenomenon made evident in this way but it is nature's way of continuing the process. It is for this reason that I see for the future an increasing preoccupation with the way human beings conduct themselves. There is an increasing interest in studies that would inform us of what is taking place in our own evolution. It could be of great value if we were informed of what is occurring at levels below or beyond our consciousness. Is the evolutionary process moving us toward becoming more human or less human? I have the impression that we are becoming more human even though there is ample evidence of inhuman behavior. We can, and often do, rationalize our inhuman or inhumane response, but what of our human or humane responses? What do they represent, where do they stand in nature in the process of evolution? Are they evolutionary or devolutionary? Are they likely to increase the probability of human survival, prolong human survival and human evolution on the planet, or foreshorten them? It seems clear that a strong reaction is developing among those who are more humane to alter the way human beings conduct themselves. The amount and kind of inhuman, or inhumane, behavior that goes on at all levels and in so many different ways makes it clear to me that there is a need to identify it as well as to identify the countervailing or correcting influences. It would seem, therefore, that an examination, from an evolutionary point of view, of what is called humane behavior is now required.

This must be seen not only from the point of view of evolution in nature (prebiological and biological) but also from the point of view of the evolution of that natural phenomenon called the human mind (metabiological). It must also be seen from the viewpoint of the evolutionary value of negative as well as of positive behavior. It must be seen not only from the point of view of the evolutionary value of similar behavior in biological evolution, but also from the metabiological, or human-life evolutionary, point of view. This begs the question as to whether human beings are becoming more or less humane. It poses the question as to whether the trend for the future is more toward humaneness or inhumaneness.

I now find the behavior of individuals to be a rich source of insight into the process of evolution, at the nonhuman as well as at the human level of complexity in which the human mind has become the dominant force in the process of evolution. It seems to me that we are now confronted with the necessity to examine phenomena associated with the human mind from an evolutionary point of view. A magnifying lens, an appropriate microscope of suitable magnitude, will be needed to examine the fine structure of human behavior in a wide variety of circumstances, in order to provide the insight into what is happening to us in evolution. We must see ourselves as the result of the evolutionary process and consider ways by which we may be able to influence the future course of human evolution. For this purpose it will be necessary to develop an evolutionary theory of human nature, to examine the relationship of the human mind to human nature in evolution, and to predict the role of the human mind in the future as well as to recognize its role in the present.

CRITERIA FOR SELECTION

Evolution is a problem-creating as well as a problem-solving process. It is an order-maintaining as well as an order-elaborating process oriented toward higher complexity. Since the process serves the need for problem-solving, and since it is both error-making and error-correcting, there must come a time when the critical factor for continuity consists in the ability for error-correcting to be more effective than the capacity for error-making. If this does not obtain, then biological survival is threatened as is any meaningful metabiological form of existence.

There are numbers of problems that arise in the course of evolution, and it seems as if the human species has reached a new stage, a new crisis in evolution. Some problems are more immediate and more threatening than others, and they are the ones to be dealt with first. Only then does it become possible to deal with the others. When, in human evolution, a number of problems present themselves simultaneously, stress is experienced in trying to deal with all of them concurrently. It is necessary to decide what not to do as well as what to do. Nature itself is not subjectively involved, but human beings are. They are torn between reactions of self-interest and reactions of community or species interest. Yet both are necessary so that the evolutionary process may continue. Thus, crises worsen if *either/or* choices have to be made. They are resolvable if *both/and* choices are possible.

I have the impression that it is *both/and* resolutions that have served as the way out of crises in the course of evolutionary time. One example of this is that a species depends upon the integrity and competence of its individual members, and the individual influences the integrity and competence of the species. Neither one nor the other alone is sufficient. Both are necessary for continued survival and evolution.

We can now see the trend that metabiological and metabiospherical evolution might favor and can see what human beings might do for their collective as well as their individual self-fulfillment. It would seem to be advantageous to recognize those individuals who possess qualities that contribute significantly to the processes of error-correcting and problem-solving on the highest level. Creativity is necessary for this purpose but not sufficient. It is essential that these attributes also be applied pragmatically to problems of critical importance.

Therefore it is in the best interest of the species, from an evolutionary point of view, for individuals with problem-solving attributes, as well as those possessing other creative and innovative traits, to be recognized. This requires an attitude and a system directed to the selection of those who would also serve the species' interest and not only the interest of the individual.

The criteria in the selection of such individuals must be examined. There is a fine line between destructive self-interest and enlightened self-interest. This distinction is of great importance in human evolution and will be recognized as a new basis for selection in human evolution. If the complexity of the human mind has emerged as a problem-solving system in the course of evolution, then it would follow that those who prove to be most effective in this respect would be selected.

It would also be well to recognize the universal yearning of the individual mind to be engaged in a purposeful way conducive to the solution of critical problems. The need for this, and the fulfillment and the satisfaction arising from nourishing this need, attest to its importance as a positive evolutionary force which atrophies if neglected. If errors of judgment and maladaptive behavior result from failing to develop and improve the use of reason and the ordering of intuition, we begin to see what should be done to correct the error of failing to develop the human mind to its full potential for serving the process of natural selection by which it has been shaped.

Thus, seeing the human mind as here presented suggests its resemblance to an ecosystem. Each individual plays a role. Each individual in the species exists in an interacting network of systems involving problem-solving according to an implicit order inherent in the selective process of evolution. If evolution is like the mind, then nature is like the body, and the two together are related in the same way as the biological and metabiological systems in the body/mind relationship.

These are different ways of perceiving evolution in nature and of perceiving the human mind in relation to nature and evolution, as well as to the human body and to human life. It is as if nature, evolution, and mind have many qualities in common and can be viewed as different ways of perceiving the basic phenomena of order and existence. These may be seen metaphysically (essense/existence) as well as physically (energy/mass), and also metabiologically (intuition/reason) as well as biologically (gene/soma). Seen in this way, they are different aspects of the same phenomena. Thus, they may be seen as identical or as different, depending upon the point of view one chooses to take. If seen from both points of view, the problem posed by the *either/or* approach is resolved by the *both/and* approach. Thus a *both/and* resolution is of a higher order.

The idea here expressed may well have implications for biological as well as metabiological systems. Philosophical and epistemological implications upon which scientific observations depend and are nourished go beyond the limits of the scientific approach that had been used for observations of the phenomena of nature, evolution, and mind, and their relationship to each other.

CONSCIOUSNESS OF EVOLUTION

Consciousness has emerged in the process of evolution. When we become conscious of evolution and become one with evolution, we become aware of cosmic order. We see physical order and metaphysical order. We see biological order and metabiological order. We see the binary structure of order. We see the unity and the diversity in nonliving and living processes. We see evolution in all of these processes and even in the process of evolution itself. Thus we see evolution as ever-evolving in the creation and manifestation of greater and greater complexity. Evolution governs everything and is both its ultimate cause and its own ultimate purpose. We can be chosen by it if we choose to serve it. It governs and selects the future from the past and the present.

What are the criteria for selection? What are the most enduring of all the many criteria that have existed earlier? What are the criteria that appear to be operating now? In what way have criteria for selection evolved in the course of evolutionary time and what criteria may prove to be relevant for selection in the future? Is this the way we can know what to do now and how to use our consciousness, a capacity which seemingly distinguishes us from all other forms of life? In what way does this impose upon us a responsibility as well as a privilege? What is our duty in the light of our trusteeship in the process of evolution? If we trust evolution, we must learn to trust ourselves, our intuition and reason. We can feel as well as know; we can know intuitively as well as cognitively. There is more than one way of knowing. We must use all of the many ways of knowing. We can know subconsciously, in sleep and in wakefulness. We can know with or without words. We can know with or without science. But we can know more with language and with science than without them. Knowing consciousness and consciousness of knowing are the means by which we can know evolution. Thus, we can know ourselves and our relationship to evolution.

Our knowledge of ourselves is in the process of evolution. We do not now see ourselves as we did earlier in human history, nor do we all see ourselves in the same way. It must be that these differences have some meaning that can be recognized. When known, or even unknown, the significance is likely to be of an evolutionary character. It will be related to the value of one view in preference to another in terms relevant to evolution. Thus, ultimately, evolutionary values will be perceived and defined and will provide the basis for human values. Human values and evolutionary values are integrally related to each other. What will prove to be of evolutionary value will be seen to be of human value, and what will be of human value will also be of value in terms of the process of evolution.

In this way dogmatic ideologies will yield to ideas and practices that are related to the fundamental necessities of human life. They will be seen and judged in terms of the unfolding of human potentiality, metabiologically and biologically. Therefore, it would seem that an evolutionary view of human life will ultimately become the basis upon which human values will be recognized and will be the determining influence on human thought and human behavior. In this way human responsibility will be determined and judged.

From this point of view it becomes possible to consider the direction of change, which develops in time and in different cultures under the different circumstances that prevail in each. It will become possible to view the future and to alter our views of ourselves by influencing the emerging future in a way that is likely to be evolutionarily advantageous.

Thus the evolutionary point of view will relate us to the universe, to each other, and allow us to discover a way of life that will increase the realization of man's highest biological and metabiological potential for consciousness and creativity, his highest hopes and aspirations. At this point in evolution such an ideal seems far away indeed. However, it also seems to be the path to follow. Only on such a path will human evolutionary potential be realized as man recognizes that he is one with evolution.

MIND

EMERGENCE OF MIND

It is as if through my mind I am in contact with nature and with evolution and thereby experience both nature and evolution. It is as if my mind is a part and an extension of both, an integral part of nature and evolution. It is a means by which I know each separately and their relationship, as well as the relationship of my mind to each in different ways. I perceive, I feel, and I think. In these ways my mind knows, my body feels, and I react to what is reflected in my mind and in my body.

The complex phenomenon of the relationship of my mind to nature and to evolution insists upon being understood. My mind seems to want to comprehend itself and its relationship to nature and to evolution as well as its relationship to other minds. It wants to understand its relationship to my body, and of my body to it. It wants to understand thinking and feeling and what they mean as an extension of nature and of evolution. It is as if there is a convergence of nature, evolution, and mind, a convergence of what I feel with what I think, what I sense with what I know, that impels me to reconcile and consciously comprehend these processes.

It is as if this is all occurring at a level of my mind that I sense to be beneath consciousness and that seems to want to merge with my conscious mind. At the moment when the two converge, when they commune, I feel a rush of ecstasy, a sense of release, of satisfaction, and of fulfillment. This is also experienced when deeply meaningful relationships are made or renewed. It is an experience not unlike that which occurs in response to an action which we seem to be impelled by nature, by evolution, to consummate. It is an experience not unlike that which occurs when we achieve a necessary goal, whether it be of value in terms of nature, evolution, or in terms of our own minds. Each has its own criteria that may be different or the same and that may prove to be mutually advantageous or not.

It is as if the processes of nature, evolution, and mind lead to the development of criteria consistent with evolutionary continuity. At one time before the parts were separated from the whole, nature, evolution, and mind were one and each arose out of an undifferentiated unity. They are part of a continuum, a process of long duration that will endure into the future. This process existed before the emergence of human consciousness and will continue long after.

However, the emergence of human consciousness constitutes a nodal point in the process of evolution, the significance of which may not be immediately apparent. It must be reflected upon, once its existence is experienced. It is as if feeling precedes thinking, although thoughts, or the seeds of thoughts, can arise in the mind in sleep, and in dreams, simultaneously with feeling. This depends upon the way the mind works and the presence of consciousness in relation to the body, the state of receptivity as well as sensitivity of both mind and body. To the extent to which nature, evolution, and mind are in tune will the music of nature be experienced and transmitted to the conscious mind as well as to other minds by whatever means of communication may exist, biologically or metabiologically, or by whatever other means of communication may have evolved in the biosphere and the metabiosphere.

The emergence of man, and the emergence of the human mind, may be seen as serving the evolutionary process. Seen in this way, those human minds that are in tune with the evolutionary process seem to have an anticipatory sense—a sense of what is needed for continuity. It is for this reason that aptitude and creativity must be present. This is also the meaning of the value placed upon "adaptitude" in the form of innovation and competence in coping with the conditions for evolution and survival.

INTUITION AND REASON

The evolution of the human mind, of consciousness, depends upon the evolution of intuition and reason. It is important to recognize the binary nature of this relationship and to focus upon intuition and upon reason separately and together, observing how they work, first in particular individuals and then in all individuals. This will lead to the observation that some have more or less highly developed intuitions, ones that are more or less adapted to dealing with present and future reality. The same may be said about reason or reasoning.

A new way of thinking is now needed to deal with our present reality, which is sensed more sensitively through intuition than by our capacity to observe and to reason objectively. Our subjective responses (intuitional) are more sensitive and more rapid than our objective responses (reasoned). This is in the nature of the way the mind works. We first sense and then we reason why. Intuition is an innate quality, but it can be developed and cultivated.

The evolutionary way of thought might be seen as the intuitive way of thought. Intuition may be seen as a continuation or extension of "natural" processes, like instinct, for example. Reason may be seen as that which man adds to explain his intuitive sense. Intuition *and* reason play a powerful role in our lives and it is necessary, therefore, to understand each separately and together.

Intuition must be allowed free rein and be allowed to play. Only then do we select, from among the patterns that emerge, the intuitively arising basis on which to contribute to metabiological and metabiospheric evolution. The intuitive mind establishes the parameters, the premises on the basis of which reason is formulated to correspond to intuitively perceived patterns.

The intuitive and reasoning realms operate separately and together. It is necessary to educate and to cultivate each separately, and both together. I suspect that if appropriately cultivated, the two would work best together if the intuition were liberated from bondage and constraints, and put in charge of a respectful intellect. If a respectful intellect becomes conscious of intuition and reflects upon what it observes, a self-correcting, self-modifying and self-improving process is established.

This suggests the pattern of the way the mind works as a feeling/thinking entity, as an entity with an intuition/reason system for guidance. This is a way to regard how the mind functions, as a self-organizing, self-developing system which possesses a means for feedback, and also for feedforward, serving the process of metabiological evolution. This system must have emerged by chance and was then selected for its self-correcting and self-balancing as well as its self-selecting and self-organizing properties. To perform in this way is in the mind's own self-interest and in the self-interest of those human beings which it serves, and in the interest of the evolutionary process itself.

Most human beings do not see themselves, or their minds, as serving the process of evolution. Nevertheless, it would represent a major phase change in the evolution of human consciousness for such a realization to occur and to be acted upon. At this point in our evolution, as we further cultivate the human mind, we are becoming more and more aware of the role and the importance of intuition and reason in human evolution as well as in everyday life.

UNITARY VISION

One of the many phenomena associated with the phenomenon of the human mind is thinking. It is as if there is a will, independent of us, and yet part of us, that is preoccupied with such questions. Although systems of thought about such questions and systems of explanation have been developed throughout historical time, the human mind seems constantly to be preoccupied in reflecting upon its own existence as well as upon the universe.

This process has been going on ever since the human mind emerged in the course of evolution. Thus I see the continuity of what I am doing and of what I am reflecting upon. I see the activity that is going on in my mind as continuous with the process of evolution. Therefore I see all that exists relative to all else in a unified way, a way that suggests the nature of the relationship of matter, nonliving and living, to matter that has become conscious of itself. Seen in this way, human matter, or the human mind, is perceived as part of an evolutionary continuum. It has the capacity to reflect upon itself and upon its origin, its roots in the past and its potentiality for the future.

These questions will continue to be asked and reflected upon long into the future, just as they have been in the past. The form of the question reflects what is known, believed, or surmised at different periods in human history and in human development. Of what value, therefore, is another statement, another set of personal reflections upon questions that can only be appreciated by the mind? The proof of the validity of such observations, as may be seen in these imaginings, can come, at best, from a complementary examination of subjective and objective experience, from a complementary examination of the epistemology of science and of human experience.

It would seem that it is necessary to accept both kinds of experience as related so as to develop a set of perceptions about the mind as it exists in reality. In this way subjectively arising experiences of the mind, together with their examination and evolution, can be used to enlarge and enrich the experience of the mind itself.

I do not deal here with the question of mind in neurophysiological terms, in terms of what actually happens in the brain in the process of thinking or imagining, or in any of the intuitive or cognitive events which we have all experienced. Rather I refer to what I have experienced and the meaning of these experiences in terms of the process of evolution, in the course of which all of the manifestations of nature emerged, one of which is the phenomenon of the human mind.

VALUES—INDIVIDUAL AND SOCIETAL

We seem to have a powerful need to succeed, to excell, and to be chosen. It takes a variety of forms. We are driven by the force of this phenomenon, which seems to be linked to seeking and choosing what is advantageous. An animal is chosen for evolution by its health. A healthy animal would be expected to choose what is evolutionarily advantageous, what leads to survival and selection. In the same way, the system of rewards and the social and cultural attitudes of human beings will have an important influence on values and behavior. Thus, social and cultural attitudes play an important role in value systems which have a determining effect upon behavior, and thus upon human evolution.

Fear and greed are complex phenomena that can be used to activate people's minds and cause them to behave in ways not necessarily in their best interest, or to behave in ways that are in their best interest. The ability to make this distinction and to act appropriately varies widely among individuals and among groups. These basic qualities, which have evolutionary importance, are powerfully significant in human as well as in other evolutionary systems. In human beings the mind also has a modulating and a determining influence upon the emotions associated with greed and fear and therefore upon behavior. Thus it may be possible to influence the mind to react and to process information and experience in a way that would prove to be advantageous, i.e., healthy. In a similar way we can speak of such qualities as balance or wisdom. However, each of these involves a judgment, even a prejudgment, as to what is advantageous and in accordance with values, and system of rewards. The system of rewards in a society, as well as the dominant value system, is an important determinant of individual values.

This clarifying idea has value in relation to a number of universal questions. However, are we clear about which qualifies we value and wish to reward so as to influence and thereby affect attitudes and behavior? This kind of influence on the direction of human evolution is critical. This is what mankind needs to clarify at present. This is what mankind desires unconsciously, but this is not what is being questioned by most people. However, I believe that a few extraordinary human beings already are aware of this and know what mankind needs.

The metabiological, socio-metabiological, and sociocultural environments have a profound influence upon the function of the individual's mind and his behavior. Behavior will be determined by many physical and bodily factors as well as by mind-related events. It is necessary to know how to distinguish between the two and how to deal with each separately as well as together. This is the process of thought concerning the role and value of laws restricting, for example, the use of guns, tobacco, alcohol, drugs, and other disadvantageous practices. The value of education, physical health, and human development also becomes our concern. These examples illustrate the importance of thought in relation to human qualities not only in terms of survival but also in terms of evolution. There must be such a thing as advantageous evolution as well as advantageous survival. We need to emphasize the former more than has been done. It is necessary to recognize the need for self-selection as a way to initiate the process of self-selection and its influences upon the direction and character of the pattern of selection.

It is important to consider initiation as part of the phenomenon of emergence in the process of evolution and to understand how it functions so that it may be consciously practiced. Thus, we are addressing ourselves to the question of the factors involved in the process of evolution and to the way in which this process determines evolutionary direction. It would then become possible to understand how this process could be influenced by those we might call the trustees of evolution.

If the key to the future is through the talents of individuals, then it will be necessary to develop methods for their selection and conditions for their cultivation. We must therefore become more precise about what we mean as well as about the methods for achieving these ends. As we consider these questions and continue to devote ourselves to the need to develop human talent, it becomes clear that it is to our mutual advantage to do so so that society may benefit. This concept has the quality of human self-interest but not that of a particular vested-interest group. It requires a different attitude from what presently prevails, a different way of evaluating human beings and their minds.

Such an attitude becomes more precise as a society defines and acts upon a consciously established value. If we focus upon this idea until it penetrates deeply and becomes firmly fixed in our minds, we begin to see the importance of the human mind and its cultivation. It will be necessary to recognize the significance of concern for the spectrum of values that prevails and the effect this has upon the quality of human minds in various cultures.

If equal value is placed upon value to society and value to the individual, then, in time, we will be able to combine the two and eventually we will find that one feeds the other. This merging would have the effect of altering the value structure of a culture and would encourage a change that could be advantageous for individual creativity as well as for society. It would also favor extraordinary individuals and especially those whose creativity is related to the value of creativity in itself, to its cultivation in a way that would be of benefit to society. This is an example in which the question of self-interest can be examined and seen in terms of mutual interest. It also justifies a reorientation of our value structure and the structure of our relationships. The assumption that all individuals are guilty of greed and selfishness at the expense of others, and that generosity and altruism are unnatural states, is a disadvantageous premise for society.

This brings us to the basic issue concerning our perception of human nature and the predominant view about the fundamental characteristics of human beings. It is evident that most people are self-protective but some are destructive to themselves as well as to society. Nevertheless, if it becomes possible to have a positive and constructive influence upon individual human values and therefore upon the values adopted by society, this, in turn, would have a positive effect upon the dominant value structure in a culture.

THE EVOLUTIONARY PATH

Those who consider such questions are confronted with considering a basis for a pedagogy, a belief system, and a cosmogony appropriate for our time in human history and human evolution. The basis for these lies in the newly emerging reality of human experience, including changing conditions for the human species and discoveries brought forth by scientific knowledge. All belief systems, or bases of pedagogy, religion, and cosmogony, arise within the human mind, in the interactions between minds, and also in the course of various kinds of experience. These, then, determine behavior based upon the resulting belief/knowledge systems. At first there is a great deal of belief; as time goes on, knowledge increases and the belief/knowledge ratio changes. The two may be said to be in constant interaction but have been in opposition —opposition that has been the cause of wars ever since different belief systems and different systems of knowledge have existed.

If one were to compare the human animal with all other forms of life, it would be evident that there has emerged, with the appearance of the human mind, a system with as much diversity as was seen after the appearance of life out of inorganic matter. Thus a leap similar to the emergence of life itself occurred when the human mind appeared in the course of evolution. The same may be said about the events that followed the appearance of prebiological matter. A qualitative change occurred at each of these moments in evolutionary time and a similar change seems to be developing with the increasing complexity of consciousness. The effect is still not fully manifest. It will depend upon many forces that are at play. All cannot be known in advance but many can be discerned and anticipated from patterns of human behavior and by comparison with the behavior of prior forms of matter that previously appeared in the course of evolution, especially other forms of life but even nonliving matter.

By seeing all this in evolutionary perspective, it becomes possible to observe the continuity from the moment when the cosmos emerged from randomness. We can also recognize the discontinuities that appeared in the course of the process of the evolution of matter in its various forms.

We are now at a divide in the evolutionary path. We have the possibility to increase and use our consciousness of the new reality confronting us. We have the opportunity to become conscious of wisdom, of all the other phenomena relevant to our survival, and of our unfolding in the process of evolution. This consciousness will take time to emerge and diffuse through the population of mankind now existing in the many different cultures and subcultures on earth. This is the way the process of evolution operates in all phenomena. All that we may be able to do is to influence its direction and facilitate the process through our cooperation in ways that remain to be discerned or discovered. Thus we may determine the feasibility and effectiveness of the evolutionary way of thought and of the evolutionary process in everyday life.

Stated in this way the human condition appears to be almost hopeless, without the possibility of avoiding the destruction of human history and human evolution in ways predicted by the doomsayers. However, it is interesting to contemplate ways by which this kind of an evolutionary outcome can be altered. The outcome is uncertain but the issues with which we are confronted are compelling. The question remains as to whether or not we can influence human destiny constructively. It seems evident that if anything can be done, it will involve influences acting upon the human mind. It will require that the human mind act upon itself, in the sense that the minds of human beings act upon each other.

All of this will have to be recognized and understood. Certain experiences will be necessary to cause this to take place. There is now sufficient empirical knowledge to suggest that it may be possible, under given circumstances, to create the constructive effect. An understanding of the nature of the phenomena involved is required both to ascertain the causes and effects and to conceive of means for resolving the human predicament. It is for this reason that a natural basis is required for a system of pedagogy, a religion, and a cosmogony that are adaptable to the realities we face at present as well as in the future.

OUR SENSORY SYSTEM

Since sense organs exist for commitments and responsibilities, then we should be disturbed in sleep, as well as at other times, when these commitments and responsibilities remain unfulfilled. Our emotions are engaged. We are infused with feelings of sympathy or anger, depending upon our internal states and what people do to us and to and for each other. Some are in tune with each other and tend to react similarly even at distances. We seem to respond to a need to apply our knowledge in order to deal with urgent problems, to collaborate with evolution by correcting and improving the human condition as necessity, and not only as personal choice, demands. Our sense of justice, truth, integrity, and responsibility is activated. We feel impelled to alleviate suffering. The existence of sophisticated means of communication has the effect of creating feelings of disturbance even at long range when acts of horror and violence are reported, however far away. Our sense organs make us aware of relationships, responsibilities, and commitments which exist unconsciously or consciously. This may be the way the mind works and may be the process by which human kind plays its role in evolution.

Thus our common humanity, our connections with each other, our hopes and aspirations, may be stronger than we realize and may be more actively stimulated because of the state of the world, as well as the present stage of our evolution. It is as if this is the process of human evolution itself. It demonstrates the effects of environments and the different effects that different kinds of people have on each other. It also explains the effects of different kinds of relationships and circumstances on relationships. It explains what I mean by "relationship, the fifth dimension." It suggests that we are aware of four dimensions: the three dimensions of space and the dimension of time. We are aware of that to which we are related, or those to whom we are related, whether this be known consciously or unconsciously. This would mean that we would be as much disturbed by what occurred in such relationships as we would by changes in our relationships to gravitation, or by changes in time, through acceleration or deceleration, or through changes in us such as disturbances in our biological rhythms. Thus, in the same way, we begin to know about the extent to which a sense of time is built into us, even into our molecules that pulsate rhythmically.

This explains why people are moved to protest the absence of, infringements upon, and threats to human rights and human life wherever these may exist in the world. This is why we react negatively to reports of atrocities and to inhumane events in revolutions, as well as to other forms of terrorism wherever they occur.

It is as if this is now in the air we breathe; it is in the air we hear (radio) and in the air we see (television). We cannot escape the effects upon us. However, there are some who are more sensitive than others and who have ways of knowing that something is "wrong," or "not right"; and thus they are impelled to action. These cognizant human beings seem to serve directly the evolutionary process of correction and improvement.

Those with such sensitivity and with such built-in consciousness would be expected to have different sensitivities and different knowledge from those whose sensibilities are less pronounced. It would follow, therefore, that people can be motivated toward improving the human condition, if it is possible to move them in ways that they already sense intuitively and about which they may be activated to know consciously and then to act constructively. Thus we need to be sensitive to opportunities as well as to dangers so as to increase the probability that we will act and react creatively when confronted by particular circumstances and opportunities. This is a way of taking advantage of the sensitivities that exist in the human organism by which human evolution proceeds. These are the mechanisms by which family relationships function, by which encouragement and affirmation are offered, and by which creativity fulfills human life.

All this is mediated by the way the mind functions and reveals the importance of the mind and the necessity that more and more attention be given to the mind system. When attention was given to the immune system, it had a powerful effect in improving the human condition, human health, and human well-being. The equivalent of this is now needed for the mind system, but it is a far more complex problem than exists in relation to the immune system and its manipulation for enhancing human health and human well-being. Analogous understanding of the mind system would require attention to many different mind-related functions such as values, attitudes, and behavior. This enters the metabiological realm as distinct from the biological, in which the immune system resides. However, the biological and metabiological realms are in contact and communication with each other, as evidenced by the existence of what is now being called the psychoneuroimmunological axis. It is evident that relationships which are metabiological affect us biologically, and that biological changes affect us metabiologically.

There is still a great deal to be learned about the mind, about mind-related phenomena, and how they function, before we become sufficiently aware of our minds, of the minds of others, and of our relationships and the needs pertaining to these relationships, so as to be able to improve our lives individually and collectively.

INFLUENCES ON MIND

We all have many more sensitivities than we know. More things affect us without our conscious awareness, or concern, and make a difference to us, than we notice. We often realize this only when something changes, or has been taken out of place. We are aware of noises and of sounds. We are affected by music or by silence. We feel differently when we are in the center of a city, in the mountains, or at the seashore. We feel differently in a cathedral or a museum, in a department store or at a rodeo or in a hospital. The environment or the context of our lives affects us. We feel culture shock when going from one cultural milieu to another, whether from New York to Paris, from Africa to Scandinavia, from the city to the country. We become aware that we care, that we are sensitive to what happens to other human beings, to the way they are treated. We do or do not identify ourselves with others. We feel for them and with them. We sense all this in many different ways. We are reminded of our feelings. We can sense what it must be like to be in someone else's place. We are moved by seeing a blind person cross a street in traffic and by seeing two blind people leaning upon each other, or a lame person leading one who is blind.

We are affected by a thief, by one who deliberately deceives us. We are troubled by those who create in us disagreeable moods and we are soothed by those who are pleasant and agreeable. All these different sensations take place whether or not we are aware of their cause.

All this is sensed and communicated and, therefore, we are in contact with more people than we realize. We are more or less sensitive to more or fewer people at different times and even at different times of the day. We are affected by our surroundings in wakefulness and in sleep. We are constantly in touch with everything that touches us when we reach out or are reached.

All this occurs unconsciously as well as consciously. We are more often unconscious and unaware of what affects us and we are constantly trying to become more and more comfortable, often reacting to our discomfort in negative rather than positive ways, evoking negative rather than positive responses, whether from family or from colleagues, from friends or from people we do not know. All this is communicated and recommunicated. It affects others as well as ourselves.

We are in a sea of sensations. We are immersed in a context that contains us and we are as much in contact with one another as if we were bathed in the same body of water. We are enveloped in the same air, in the same atmosphere of emanations, whether solar, stellar, or human. We are affected in similar ways even though we may react differently. We react in ways that are affected by the way we perceive. We are affected by what we hear and by what we are told. We are moved according to how we interpret all of this and by what it means to us, whether it seems threatening or reassuring, disturbing or quieting. We are as sensitive in many ways as a bird in a tree or a wolf in the forest. We feel more than we know. We sense former times as we are reminded of past events, past circumstances. We have a sense of the future and a greater or lesser capacity to apprehend what might happen at some future time. We have all these capacities; we react in our minds and our bodies in a variety of ways. We have a greater or lesser capacity to cope with our inner and our outer experiences. We are caught between two worlds, the world of our minds and the world we inhabit. Each affects the other since they are parts of the same whole, since they are one.

We are touched by, and in touch with, everything around us and even at some distance from us. We can ascend and descend as well as transcend with our minds. We can do many more things in our minds than with our bodies. What is done with the body is often more visible than what is done in the mind, although the mind is involved in what the body does and the body is involved in what the mind does. It seems, therefore, that the mind and the body are complementary. Each without the other would be incomplete and therefore more importance cannot be given to one than to the other. The two in harmony are capable of the most extraordinary feats. If we are aware of this, we are able to know our capacities, to test our limits as well as our potentialities. We come to know ourselves as we are related to others. We become aware that we are not alone, that we are dependent and interdependent. Our minds and our imaginations then begin to open and we are in touch with a wider world than we ever knew existed.

We are in touch with the minds of others, their thoughts, their imaginations, their fears and reassurances. We are disturbed or comforted, menaced or uplifted. It is for this reason that we need to be concerned with others, with how their minds work, and with the effect this has on the way they behave. All this is to say that in the world of today, we are more openly and instantly exposed to each other even over vast distances of space and through reaches of time.

We may be disturbed directly or indirectly by effects mediated through our minds or through other sensations. Nevertheless, we are affected by all with which we are in touch, directly or indirectly, and our lives, therefore, are less our own than might have been the case earlier in human evolution when there were 1 million minds or less on the face of the earth as compared to the time when there were 10 million, 100 million, or even 1 billion minds. Now there are 4.5 billion minds, on the way to becoming 10 billion. It is not surprising, therefore, that in the short time during which we have gone from a few million to many billions of minds on the face of the earth, we have not yet learned to adapt ourselves to the rate of change which is so rapid as to exceed the capacity of many to tolerate.

If we are each in contact with so many others, it is hardly a wonder that the effects increase more geometrically than arithmetically. We are more often disturbed than quieted for reasons related to the relatively greater number of minds. We often seek surcease in various ways; we seek comfort or a way to feel less disturbed. We often seek the comfort of other minds, or the balance of activities, or the solace of music, or of drugs, or even of vengeance against those we feel to be the source of our discomfort or plight.

How do we manage in a world such as this, a world that is new to the species as a whole and certainly to each of its parts, which are affected in different ways and which have more or less evolved to cope with the changes in circumstances for which they may not at all be responsible and the cause of which they may be unaware? This kind of mind problem is different in some respects from, and yet similar in other respects to, the kinds of mind problems with which humans have been confronted in the past. What is of importance is the necessity to identify the mind-related nature of the problems with which human beings are confronted today. Threats of the past may have been related more to physical existence. Now it appears that threats are related more to our minds and to the integrity of our minds, which are more readily and easily assaulted even than our bodies. Therefore, the mind, which is more open to invasion, is more vulnerable than any other part of our bodies. We have all kinds of defense mechanisms to maintain the integrity of our bodies; we can cover, protect, withdraw, hide. But in relation to our minds this is more difficult to accomplish. We can immunize and fortify our bodies. But what is the equivalent for our minds? We are, in effect, parts or elements of the collective mind of humankind even though we have the illusion of being enclosed in our respective body-spaces. Nor are we isolated from others who have gone before us or from those who are to follow, any more than we are isolated from our contemporaries, near or far.

Thus we are called upon to recognize the plight of others as well as our own in our own self-interest. We can no longer consider ourselves as protected from others merely by shutting ourselves off or by withdrawing. That possibility no longer exists, since the barriers have been broken by means of accessibility and communication that reaches us as if infusing the air we breathe. We are at one with the atmosphere we inhale as we are with the atmosphere into which we exhale. We and all others inhale and exhale the same atmosphere, whether it be the air we breathe or the thoughts and feelings we share. Therefore, it is as much in the interest of each as of all to improve the health, in mind and in body, of each and of all at a time when we are so numerous and so closely linked. It is as necessary to be concerned about our neighbors, near or far, as it is to be concerned with ourselves and our kith and kin. This is a new state in the world, a new reality with which we must contend. We can no longer consider ourselves alone, nor can we relate to ourselves without regard for our relationship to others. Our minds are in touch, our minds are linked and are interrelated.

METABIOLOGICAL HEALTH

Although the power of the mind to heal itself and to restore itself is great, training and experience are needed to master this power. Just as the mind needs nourishing food and a nourishing diet biologically and metabiologically, so it can be malnourished and even poisoned. When this occurs, its capacity to self-regulate and to self-heal is impaired and may be destroyed, resulting in various kinds of pathological manifestations. The capacity to self-regulate, to self-heal, and to self-renew may be one of the most important functions of the mind not only for itself but also in relation to others. There must be a capacity for some minds to nourish and to heal others, and some minds provide this function, protecting both self and society.

There are different sources of health and of ill health, for both the mind and the body. If this is true, health and illness need to be dealt with. There is a need for understanding the human responsibility for mind-health or mind-illness in order to deal with this most important of all natural phenomena.

In the evolutionary process we are confronted with a new reality, a new challenge and opportunity. In the face of this, I recognize the great danger that exists if we fail to strengthen and use the health-making and health-restoring power of the mind. This is the most difficult task for the mind to perform, especially for that mind which is already malformed or malfunctioning. However, quality of healing may well be the most important thing to focus upon, since the mind's own health and well-being depend upon itself and upon others, especially if self-help is not enough.

It may well be the function of the phenomenon of mind to keep individual minds as fit as possible. It is analogous to what exists in the ecosystem of the molecules and cells of the body. It may be useful to accept the analogy between what we know about the body health of the individual and of the species in its various social, political, and economic manifestations, and mind-health, so as to determine how best to deal with both the strength and weakness of the mind. Thus it is clear that it is important to be able to recognize a healthy mind, and to observe its effect upon itself and upon others, and also to recognize what impairs or destroys the health of a healthy mind. This health is delicately balanced, and when disturbed the balance can be restored by a harmonious mind-body relationship, self-maintained or with the help of others.

There is a challenge to understand how such relationships work both individually and collectively. There is a great need to develop a better understanding of the mind and of relationships from a metabiological point of view and to develop a basis for understanding metabiological health. This point of view can be based upon what is already known of the nature of the human mind.

There are different kinds of roles and functions each individual tends to play in the healthy functioning of the metabiosphere and in the healthy functioning of individual minds and the collective mind. This is a useful and fruitful way to appreciate the mind, evaluate its needs, and discern what can be done through human experience. In this process some carry a greater burden than others.

Seen in this way, the problem is difficult but one that can be dealt with so as to increase the probability of enlarging our knowledge of the mind and its application at a time when it would make the greatest difference to human life and society. But first each must try to heal, or repair, his own mind, a challenge that is as difficult as it is imperative.

EMERGENCE

THE PROBLEM

To many, humankind seems hopelessly sick. I can see why it has been concluded in the past that there is a need for a messiah, for someone who can heal or bring wholeness to the collective human mind. It is difficult enough to bring wholeness even to a single mind, let alone the collective mind. Too much pathology already exists in individual minds among the four and a half billion minds on the earth today, with the number increasing daily. This has the effect of increasing the amount and the proportion of imbalance still further.

I can see that if a messiah were to appear, he or she would not be long lived, being an easy target of hatred, malice, and envy. The conditions that prevail today are not healthy for saviors. One with the capacity for redeeming humankind would be wise enough to know that it cannot be done directly, but only by the indirect means of the healing of each individual. It would follow from this that a wise messiah, or one who desired to help, would not reveal himself or herself but would attempt to function as a quiet healer of the minds of human beings, a healer of the organism of humankind.

Now that I have probed the anatomy of reality, including the state of mind of human beings at this point in our development, it is clear to me that the degree of pathology is such as to make the future inauspicious unless health-creating individuals and groups arise in sufficient number and coalesce into a powerful force. They would have the capacity to counter the effects of the internally arising metabiological and sociometabiological pathogenic influences which are responsible for the present state of humankind.

What hope is there that such a phenomenon could occur? Do such individuals exist, and can they come together in sufficient strength to produce such an effect?

This question must now be faced if we are to entertain any

hope that the present trend can be diminished and ultimately reversed. If it can be, the effect would be miraculous. If it cannot be, then there will be either gradual or rapid progress toward madness, and a loss of any hope that the process could be ameliorated and cured. At moments it seems that the odds are more in favor of the trend toward disintegration. I sometimes feel that we may not be able to reverse rapidly enough the tendency toward massive madness.

Whatever hope exists lies in the capacity of individuals and groups of individuals to protect and enhance their individual and collective health, mentally (metabiologically) as well as physically (biologically). There seems to be no way through direct confrontation to save a species from self-destruction. Only through evolution will a new variety of human beings arise with the qualities of mind necessary for survival and for continued evolution beyond the stage revealed by the human mind in its present form.

Like the dinosaurs, many predominant metabiological forms with dinosaurian qualities will disappear. Then there will appear the equivalent of their successors, the birds, with qualities and capacities to live under circumstances which could not support the dinosaurs.

In the case of human beings, we will have contributed to the creation of the conditions for our own destruction by our insatiable greed, by the inability of our minds to inhibit our self-destructive tendencies. As this continues, the effect will be to segregate those with the ability to regulate their behavior themselves from those unable to do so. Those who have that capacity will survive; those who do not will be destroyed.

Healthy human beings must be mindful of this, finding ways and means for self-protection so that they may persist long enough to become the dominant force of what survives of the organism of humankind. Their task will be to recreate the ecosystem in a form that will allow it to repopulate an otherwise destroyed planet, in the midst of which there could arise oases or gardens of life altogether different from life as we know it today.

I believe that in this process we would see the emergence of small groups that would form sociometabiological islands of sanity to protect themselves from the others until such time as they may become sufficiently dominant to be safe in the context they will create.

Only through the evolution of the human mind can human beings develop in a way that will endure beyond this chaotic time. However, the first need will be to prevent the destructive from destroying the constructive, and from destroying the entire human race. This first condition must be met before it becomes possible to consider building further a better world in which to live.

Before we continue to build, we will need to know what kind of world is most appropriate and what kind of people will inhabit it. It will be necessary therefore to think in terms of a longer-range future than we do today. Those who have the capacity to do so, *and* to learn to live in a dynamic state of well-being in the present, will be among those who will have evolved to give rise to those who will survive to continue to evolve in the future.

Thus the world is presently divided between those who will be favored by evolution and those who will not be. There is little to be done for those who do not have the capacity to heal themselves and to contribute to a healthier and more fulfilling future. A great deal needs to be done to counteract their ill effects, and this is the major challenge confronting human beings and the organism of humankind which will give rise to the metabiological subspecies out of which the dominant sociometabiological subspecies of humankind will arise in the future.

It is not now possible to describe in any detail the conditions that will then prevail for survival and for continued evolution. However, they can be imagined and serve as a basis upon which many different experiments will be conducted, by individuals and groups, in an effort to solve the present problems for the future based upon an anticipation of what now seems likely and even inevitable if we are to succeed.

If this is a reasonable evaluation of the conditions that prevail at the present time, and of the prevalent direction and trends, it remains for individuals and groups to conceive of ways and means to separate themselves, to protect themselves, from the growing madness and to prepare themselves for what will be possible when the madness is dissipated and a healthier state of mind prevails in a totally transformed world.

Survival of the world as we know it is not possible. The world will have to be transformed and evolve for continued survival. This is the necessity and the imperative of our time and will continue to be so long into the future until this transformation has been achieved, or until there is no longer any hope that it may be possible.

A NEW COSMOGONY

The remedy for the human predicament, for the malfunctions in the human condition, lies in the reconciliation of the intuitive and the reasoning powers of human beings. Intuition is part of human nature; it is an expression of human nature. Its alliance with reason is an expression of what human beings have been given by nature to further the process of evolution. This innate capacity for intuition and reason emerged through the process of evolution itself. In that process, qualities that serve life and knowledge have been selected and transmitted.

Until now the important and great intellectual contributions have concerned the development of logic relating to our perception of the world and the universe in which we live. Now the problem is the development of an understanding of the mind, which has conceived all this and the evolutionary purpose that it must serve. Until this point in time the question of its purpose has not been as important as it has now become. The development of knowledge has tended to diminish the burden of sustaining physical life; now knowledge may well become one of our greatest burdens and may become so autonomously self-serving as to become separated from the innate evolutionary purpose of the human mind. It is necessary, therefore, to reexamine the present trends in the evolution of human knowledge, including those in science and technology, reconsidering the relationship between knowledge and life, between knowledge and wisdom.

Science and knowledge are essential to human life. Science for its own sake also serves human needs. Life without science and science without life are impossible at this point in human evolution because of the extent to which we have grown dependent upon science and technology. Our dependence is now so complete that we must find a way to allow the evolutionary forces to help establish the balance necessary for the healthy evolution of science in relation to human life and the creative human spirit.

It is necessary to study the evolution of intuition and reason as revealed humanistically in the evolution of our perception of ourselves. We need to evaluate the great insights of religious as well as intellectual leaders, those who represent the mutational events in metabiological evolution as manifested in religion, science, and philosophy. There is a need for a reconciliation of religion and science, just as it is necessary to reconcile intuition and reason, experience and knowledge.

By methods other than reason alone we must explore all aspects of reality in each of the many forms in which it is experienced, internally as well as externally, subjectively and objectively, intuitively as well as by observation. Through reason and the methods of science alone we are inadequately equipped to deal with the present problems of metabiological evolution. We are in need of intuition and a new cosmogony, a natural cosmogny, one that is compatible with both the epistemology of science and the epistemology of human experience.

The task with which we are confronted is much larger than merely understanding intuition and reason alone. The task is to be informed by these means and sources, and to act out in everyday life the precepts whereby the evolutionary process continues to function, continues to give birth to new forms and to eliminate others. An ethic and a morality based upon evolutionary principles are required for establishing a humane basis for human existence and for serving the process of evolution itself. It is as if this, too, is in the process of evolution in response to the necessities of life. Now the time has come for a new ethic, a new morality, for the evolutionarily significant change through which humankind is passing.

INDIVIDUAL MUTUALISM

We are in need of a new philosophy, a new ideology, on the basis of which to organize ourselves in the future. This new philosophy, or ideology, might be called individual mutualism. It requires the collective to respect the individual and individuals to participate mutually in the collective. The same idea is shared in many different ways by religions and cosmogonies the world over; many of these were appropriate in the past but are no longer as useful now as they were when first conceived.

The needs of our time are quite different from those of times past. We are in need of an altogether new and different guiding philosophy if we are to use our energy and our resources efficiently and effectively to bring about the fundamental and essential changes called for in the present state of human evolution. The need is for a global change and not merely a regional change. Something as profound as this, however, cannot occur overnight, nor even in one generation; it will require many generations, and it will differ in different parts of the world depending upon the stage in metabiological as well as biological evolution in the different cultures and societies and nations that presently exist. It will take a long time for well-established habits and practices and belief systems to change, as it will take a long time for fears, hatreds, and mutual mistrust to be alleviated.

Thus, it is clear that the amelioration of the human condition must be viewed from a long-term evolutionary perspective and that there are many things that can begin to be done to move in the direction of one of the natural outcomes that can be conceived and that might universally be preferred. However, the hazards and dangers that prevail, and which will persist for some time to come, are of such nature that it will be necessary to maintain a strict surveillance and to work actively to avoid the damage and to reduce the waste associated with the amount of destructive potential that presently exists the world over.

It seems to me that a beginning must be made to increase consciousness of where we are in human or metabiological evolution. In addition, a beginning must be made to put into practice a philosophy or an ideology that will be expressed in everyday life and not merely in an ideal to be achieved at some indefinite time in the future. It is something that must be attained piecemeal, in small amounts, by degrees. Therefore, a beginning must be made to turn ourselves even by a fraction of a degree in the direction in which we seem to want to go, though, at times, we appear to wander from the path that would lead us there. It is in search of guidance from within ourselves that consciousness is invoked in the service of coguiding and coauthoring our own evolution.

CONSCIOUS EVOLUTION

Conscious evolution will emerge from the evolution of consciousness and consciousness of evolution. Conscious evolution will result from a sufficient evolution of consciousness and a sufficiently developed consciousness of evolution. When these become adequate, then will conscious creative, metabiological evolution become apparent. Before we can engage in conscious evolution it will be necessary to further our knowledge, as well as our intuitive sense, of evolution and its relevance in human life. It will be necessary to feel and to believe that we are able to deal with our own evolution by skillfully avoiding catastrophe and moving on with a sense of responsibility for the future so that we may evolve through time at a rate limited only by the development of our consciousness of evolution.

The rate at which conscious evolution can overtake unconscious evolution will depend upon the rate at which the consciousness of evolution evolves. This development will require a change in perception, a transition from the paradigm of the systems of belief that presently prevail to a belief in conscious creative metabiological evolution as a process by which the future of humankind will be determined.

In general, living creatures live out their lives and passively contribute to the process of evolution in response to the evolutionary forces acting in them and upon them. Human beings can contribute actively (consciously) as well as passively (unconsciously) to the process of evolution. Human beings differ from other living creatures in their degree of consciousness, and their will, in their potential for creatively participating in, or contributing to, the process of biological and metabiological evolution. The two most important ways in which human beings differ from other living forms of life consist in the degree of their consciousness and in the degree of their passive/active participation in their evolution. They survive by their active participation in the process of their own evolution. This reveals the evolutionary value of consciousness.

The most meaningful activity in which a human being can be engaged is one that is directly related to human evolution. This is true because human beings now play an active and critical role not only in the process of their own evolution but in the survival and evolution of all living things. Awareness of this places upon human beings a responsibility for their participation in and contribution to the process of evolution. If humankind would accept and acknowledge this responsibility and become creatively engaged in the process of metabiological evolution consciously as well as unconsciously, a new reality would emerge, and a new age would be born.

THE PRESENT

Perhaps the essence of the crisis of our times is that we are approaching the limit of the usefulness of our knowledge of the cosmos and are now in need of turning our attention to consciousness of ourselves.

We need mirrors and magnifiers; we need to develop new ways of seeing and of recognizing ourselves. Consciousness of self and consciousness of the new reality are both necessary, and both are of the highest value for survival and evolution. They are essential for adaptation to the new reality. If we are to increase self-actualization and self-realization, self-awareness becomes an essential tool, allowing greater adaptation and wider effectiveness in dealing with and influencing the course of human experience.

It may be of value to think of consciousness and self-consciousness as two different levels of the human mind, just as we think of involuntary functions of the body in contrast to those which can be controlled by an act of will. Because of the speed of change in our times, it is imperative that we accelerate the increase in consciousness among human beings. We must become aware of the role that each of us plays and of the responsibility we have—and not merely our rights—for what happens in the present and the future.

As a species, we seem to be divided between those who dwell in the past, those who dwell in the future, and those who dwell in the present. It is obvious that it will be necessary to be concerned about each of these periods as they relate to the process of human evolution. We will need, especially, to learn how to incorporate the past into the present, how to deal with the present in terms of alternative futures, and how to choose those toward which we prefer to be oriented. This will require a new kind of thinking, an integrated and integrating approach to all aspects of our lives. We must be aware not only of details but of the context and the processes in which those details are embedded. This is the ultimate goal in human development and evolution, the ultimate purpose for the unfolding of human consciousness and of the capacity of human beings to know themselves.

The need we have now, individually and collectively, is to map our future. There are many reasons to support this idea, all related to an evolutionary perspective of human life. Other species which have survived through long evolutionary pasts have remained fixed for relatively long periods of time. In this they differ from human beings, who do not yet possess a long and stable past as a species. We are still undergoing rapid evolution, not at the biological level of complexity but rather at the metabiological level.

Our ability to anticipate the future, to plan ahead, and to make projective choices of long- as well as of short-range significance distinguishes human beings from all other living creatures. Whether or not the human species can or will colonize other places in the solar system, or beyond, is highly problematic. Regardless of our ability to do so, we possess an innate commitment to continue to improve human life on earth. Thus, as "instruments" of the evolutionary process, we are impelled to adapt and evolve. In itself, this impulse must be a built-in need in the human mind to behave in a way that is life-preserving.

In the realm of human consciousness the highest and most sophisticated form of self-regulation is based on our ability to see ahead. It requires a knowledge of self and the cosmos, and of self *in* the cosmos. The capacity exists in us, and it is one direction in which human beings are drawn. But it has to be evoked and developed. It is among the characteristics of the human being and of human consciousness which have been selected for and possess evolutionary value. The evolutionary need is to increase our breadth of consciousness as human beings, to expand our range of choice for the wisest alternatives.

This capacity to predict, to anticipate alternative consequences, is one of the most important attributes of the human mind. Exercising it enables us to avoid the worst of our possible alternatives and choose the most advantageous. This awareness can also work in such a way as to allow us to sacrifice a seeming short-term advantage for a clear long-term advantage. These attributes do not coexist equally in all minds; there is wide variation in the degree to which they do exist. Nevertheless, they are present to some extent in every individual, and it becomes of first importance to develop and apply them in our individual lives and on a larger scale for our collective benefit.

There is a human advantage to such a response; it is clearly the wisest way to behave. This sounds relatively simple. However, in practice it is not as simple as it sounds. Wisdom possesses less imperative than necessity. The mind responds more directly to necessity, especially when it is clearly advantageous for values, attitudes, and behavior to change. This seems to be the basis upon which biological evolution has proceeded and it also seems to be the basis upon which metabiological evolution must proceed.

Individuals with the greatest capacity for such behavior are likely to be among those who most effectively contributed to and thus experienced further evolution. The ability of the mind to function in this way must have been selected in the course of evolution.

The human capacity to anticipate and select will be the means whereby the future of human evolution will be determined. This will be true whether or not that power is consciously recognized. If it is not used consciously, then chance will dominate. On the other hand, if choice is exercised wisely, chance events would be used opportunistically. This second alternative requires us continually to search for, be open to, and select from those opportunities that may arise by the chance concatenation of circumstances. We will need the capacity creatively to influence changes through choice. What proceeds in the biological realm through mutation and selection proceeds in the metabiological through creation and choice.

The ability to look and to see ahead, coupled with the imperative of necessity, suggests a need at the present time for a large dose of reality and a weaning away from illusion. People have many illusions which block them from acting in their own best interest as a species, as well as individuals. In dealing with the present problems of human life, we must first be able to see the realities of our lives. Only then will it be possible to modify our lives, individually and collectively, in the ways that are necessary. It is disadvantageous to persist in old patterns when circumstances have changed and require the imminent development of new patterns.

The belief in a man-induced catastrophe or in an apocalypse, however superficially convincing, does *not necessarily* conform to what reality has in store for us in the future. It is altogether possible that the ability to look ahead, to imagine and to reason, to think, to weigh, and to judge, exists strongly enough in the minds of a sufficient number of individuals that a critical mass of minds may exist which can influence humankind to respond more appropriately than we do now.

The need to influence change consciously requires that we place as much emphasis upon process and meaning as upon chance events and choices. We must consider all events in terms of process, and in terms of possible consequences that can be anticipated. This will require the cultivation of special faculties. We will have to learn to think this way as early in life as possible, through being exposed to a world view which shapes our perception of reality in a way that affords us the greatest opportunity for growth and development. We must maintain the potential for options, for continued evolution.

We are still far away from that state of affairs. It is therefore of the greatest importance to recognize the meaning and significance this has for our everyday lives as well as for the future.

If my hypothesis is correct—if the activity of the human mind is designed to correct errors of the past and the present and invent ways for dealing with the present and the future—then it will become necessary for individuals to optimize the function of their minds toward this end. In such a context, those who have a sense of what needs to be done, what to select, and what to act upon would prove to be of the greatest value.

To use a biological metaphor, we must look upon mankind as an organism, and upon each individual as a cell. In any organism, the cells are both autonomous and functionally related: each cell has a life of its own, and simultaneously it contributes to the functioning of the total organism. There is no one officer at the top to direct the whole enterprise. Therefore each cell or individual has to do its job, contributing to its own life and the life of the organism, in order that both continue to exist. A cell is the organism's way of carrying out its functions; the organism is essential for the cell's survival. Together they form a reciprocally beneficial and interdependent relationship.

In human society as in the human body, the organism's functioning will depend upon that of its individual cells. But human communities have created collective systems which do not always take into account the real needs of the community's members, nor the individual's ability to actualize his needs. As a result we can see bureaucracies which neither acknowledge nor respond to the most central needs of their constituencies but become self-serving and pathogenic.

Society, as presently organized, should be able to deal effectively with certain kinds of errors that need to be corrected or eliminated. In many respects, however, it does not.

Error-correcting mechanisms prevent deterioration and self-destruction, and are the basis for postponing the organism's aging and death. The inability of an organism or a system to correct its errors or defects leads to dissolution, rather than to survival and evolution. The error-correcting and error-preventing mechanisms in culture, in society, in the world, are necessary to inhibit the antievolutionary forces so as to allow development to proceed.

What is needed particularly is to correct the accumulation of those errors that inhibit evolution: the unbalanced growth of population; excessive preparation for war; excessive utilization of energy; excesses leading to crime, violence, and terrorism; and excesses which have led to economic imbalance.

We need a proliferation of individuals who are capable of performing self-correcting and balancing functions. We must find a way to allow such individuals to emerge, and to merge. Such persons exist; their consciousness of their role and of their responsibility should be heightened, so that they become aware of their potentialities in order that they may then knowingly consider and choose what to do individually and collectively to contribute to this evolutionary need.

Our system for the selection of leaders who are suited to the time in which we live is no longer appropriate, useful, or effective. Individuals who are aware of this must find ways to correct this defect. What is needed are individuals who are consciously constructive rather than destructive to counterbalance the negative trends that now prevail, and to reverse them.

The principle of repair and restoration by error-correcting or error-preventing applies both to individual cells and to organisms made up of a collection of cells or individuals. The individual is important; the collective body of individuals is equally important.

The human future seems to depend heavily upon the relationships that exist among human beings. The basic needs for survival and evolution are satisfied not by existence alone but by relationships that are mutually reinforcing. We need the help of others when we have reached the limit of our capacity to help ourselves. The impulse to give help and to receive it and the desire to enter into mutually advantageous relationships are of great evolutionary value. They increase by many orders of magnitude our capacity to solve problems, and our capacity to protect ourselves and each other against adversity. We must now learn how best to defend ourselves against the threats that arise from within the organism of humankind. To this end, I see the value of developing clusters, or nodes, or networks of human beings with the mental qualities for dealing effectively with reality; for increasing awareness of reality, of nature, and of humankind; and for increasing self-consciousness and the capacity to see inwardly.

There is a vast territory which needs now to be illuminated. To do so will require the development of appropriate attitudes and techniques for the exploration of inner space. Eventually we will recognize how the mind functions for the purpose it has evolved to serve and for its adaptive role to increase the chance of survival and continued evolution. We need to identify and to choose the most advantageous options from among the many possibilities in any given situation, to strengthen our position, and to increase the chances of being chosen, of being selected in the evolutionary process. The capacity to see and to understand the option which is likely to lead to the most constructive next set of options has greater survival and evolutionary value than a more limited capacity, which might miss seeing the full range and, therefore, the path that has the greater probability of going beyond existing limitations.

This capacity to see and to understand is a basis for natural selection. It implies the capacity for healing. The principle of healing applies to society and to humankind, as well as to individuals and to tissues. The healing of the individual, and of society, will be particularly important with respect to the human mind. Focusing on the health of the mind, upon creative and healing minds, which need to be increased in number and reinforced, will repair and heal humankind as an organism. The human mind, itself sensitive and vulnerable, is in need of protection as well as of restoration to health and to wholeness.

It is of critical importance in the lives of individuals and also in the life of the species that the capacities I have referred to above be developed rapidly, lest the critical moment be lost. We can see how this operates in the lives of individuals and in the lives of groups and, on the largest scale, in the life of the human species. It is important to establish the preconditions for such behavior. It is of importance in the functioning of our minds as guardian and trustee both of our own lives and also of the species.

We are now preparing for the eventuality when the number of people on the earth is stabilized, and when there is more political and socioeconomic equilibrium than exists at the present time. Two sets of positive forces are operating at this moment—one deals with counteracting errors and dangers, the other with constructing the basis for a better future. Because these constructive forces are operating concurrently with destructive forces, the former need to be stronger, more active, and more aggressive. Individuals can bring about change more easily than can institutions. Therefore individuals are of particular importance, since they are more flexible and adaptable to changing circumstances. Institutions have greater difficulty renewing and evolving than do individuals. Therefore, it is important to focus upon the individual, and especially on individuals who possess those qualities that appear to be desirable and effectual at present.

The time will come when there will be more dynamic equilibrium in the world and, correspondingly, more balance in the minds and lives of individuals. This may well be the direction in which humankind is moving, unknowingly and imperceptibly. We can surmise that there is a conceivable point in human evolution which would correspond to the state of a mature and healthy organism in dynamic equilibrium. The mind of an individual who has reached the stage of evolutionary equilibrium would be in harmonious balance with the activities ascribed to each hemisphere of the fully developed and functioning brain. This may also be the state associated with the maximum degree of pleasurable sensation in body and mind. Even now we have begun to sense that this is the desired state.

The fear and uncertainty in our lives are a manifestation of our state of imbalance. They place us under a great stress to maintain some semblance of equilibrium; they exert an adverse effect on the health of our bodies and minds. It is as if the mind and body already know what we, the possessors of bodies and minds, do not yet understand. We human beings—social, political, economic animals that we are—have not yet recognized the nature of the dynamic equilibrium toward which we must allow ourselves to move if we are to achieve the satisfaction and fulfillment we seek.

We have not yet discovered how this can be achieved. Nor do we know the most desirable method for seeking such a state. Such knowledge can be acquired. To begin, however, we must first trace out the pattern by which this may be accomplished.

The stage will be set by the presence of a greater amount of compassion in the world, manifested by individuals. Many men and women exist now who have already understood this in their own fashion, and who have developed their way of contributing to this ideal goal. If that is the direction toward which we are moving in spite of ourselves, then it will be both efficient and effective in facilitating the process through which that movement can occur.

There is evidence to support the supposition that this may be what is happening. As a hypothesis about the direction of the future, it has the merit of being hopeful, of providing us with a goal as well as with ideas of what might be done in everyday life. The wisdom of nature will manifest itself fully when the order achieved is that of a balanced dynamic equilibrium between the forces at work in human nature and in all forms of nature, and in the relationship between them.

THE NEW REALITY

Evolution appears to be a process for dealing with new realities. The role of man in evolution appears to be to conceive and to deal with new realities consciously and creatively, that is, evolutionarily. We are now confronted by a new reality, we are moving into it inexorably as if drawn by forces beyond our control. We are drawn by the forces of evolution which have, over a long period of time, fashioned the human mind and human consciousness. The human mind is capable of anticipating and imagining the future and capable of dealing with it creatively. Those who will be selected to evolve will be the ones who possess the capacity to act wisely now and to anticipate the future.

We know all the things that are wrong, we know the dangers. We have no difficulty in seeing them and describing them. We seem to have great difficulty acting upon our intuition to save ourselves, to act in a way that, in retrospect, will be seen to have been evolutionarily sound. To be able to do so may well be an attribute possessed by relatively few, who are sufficiently evolved, who are sufficiently conscious and capable of seeing the potential forms of the future. There are few indeed who can even imagine alternative futures and can make choices of direction that would lead to the avoidance of catastrophe and the solution of problems that have arisen in the course of evolution. But such individuals do exist. It matters little that they are few in number. Only a few are needed to visualize and to initiate a process that would become self-organizing, self-propelling, and self-propagating, as is characteristic of evolutionary processes.

Our first need is to counter the antievolutionary influences and to move consciously into the next stage in human evolution. There is a qualitative difference in all aspects of this new reality. It is a new beginning. It should be seen both in terms of the opportunities that exist as well as in terms of the dangers. Both opportunity and danger exist in every crisis. The present is no exception. The best way to resolve any crisis is by choosing the path of opportunity—the evolutionarily advantageous path—and avoiding the path of danger.

It is not necessary for everyone to be conscious of the evolutionary process. It is sufficient that it be seen by a small but critical number of people. It is sufficient that the vision of conscious, creative evolution be seen by a few here and there at different levels of the population and in different parts of the world. It is necessary that this vision be shared with others, especially with the new metabiological species that is emerging in the creation of a new reality, one fashioned by the conscious choices we make now. The characteristic of this species is not one of social, political, or economic power. It is one that possesses evolutionary qualities of insight, foresight, and creativity.

Will those who follow us see us as having been good ancestors? We must ask this question of ourselves as we face the new reality. This we can do only if we project a map of the future, a map that contains all the possible futures that we can now imagine. I would conceive of some to which we would be drawn, some that will be more appealing than others.

It is clear that there is a great deal to be done by the architects of the new reality. It is clear that they will be recruited from those who can perceive the way into a more enlightened future. What is needed is a state of mind that is constructive rather than destructive.

In the course of time the ignorant, the insane, and the greedy who have assumed positions of power will be removed, and hopefully we will have the wit and the wisdom to fill these positions with architects for the better future to which people the world over aspire.

It is likely that these qualities and capacities will be found in the generation of leaders now emerging and in those who will follow. As a group they are natives of this new reality; they were born at a time when new visions had just begun to emerge. They have had to grow on their own without the benefit of traditions, for new traditions have not yet been born and the traditions of the past no longer are applicable. The basic principles of the new tradition are inherent in the old, reappearing in a new and unfamiliar form. As the old tradition was based upon the old reality, a new tradition will develop based upon the new reality. It will have greater equilibrium, and a deeper sense of humanity.

ABOUT THE AUTHOR

Dr. Jonas Salk is the Founding Director and a Resident Fellow of The Salk Institute for Biological Studies in San Diego, California. He is also Adjunct Professor in the Health Sciences at the University of California, San Diego. The institute which he founded, is dedicated not only to experimental biology but also to relating biological knowledge to philosophical and moral problems. Dr. Salk views biology both as a science and as a basic cultural discipline revealing converging relationships between man and the physical universe as well as between man and the sciences, arts, religions, and humanistic values. In his scientific work and in his writings he is the true natural philosopher.

ABOUT THE FOUNDER OF THIS SERIES

Ruth Nanda Anshen, Ph.D., Fellow of the Royal Society of Arts of London, founded, plans, and edits several distinguished series, including World Perspectives, Religious Perspectives, Credo Perspectives, Perspectives in Humanism, the Science of Culture Series, the Tree of Life Series, and Convergence. She also writes and lectures on the relationship of knowledge to the nature and meaning of man and to his understanding of and place in the universe. Dr. Anshen's book, *The Reality of the Devil: Evil in Man,* a study in the phenomenology of evil demonstrates the interrelationship between good and evil. She has lectured in universities throughout the civilized world on the unity of mind and matter and on the relationship of facts to values. Dr. Anshen is a member of the American Philosophical Association, the History of Science Society, the International Philosophical Society and the Metaphysical Society of America.